US Vehicles and Heavy Weapons of the Vietnam War

US Vehicles and Heavy Weapons of the Vietnam War

David Doyle

Pen & Sword
MILITARY

First published in Great Britain in 2021 by
Pen & Sword Military
An imprint of
Pen & Sword Books Ltd
Yorkshire – Philadelphia

ISBN 978 1 52674 364 0

A CIP catalogue record for this book is
available from the British Library.

Typeset by Mac Style
Printed and bound in India by Replika Press Pvt. Ltd.

Pen & Sword Books Limited incorporates the imprints of Atlas, Archaeology, Aviation, Discovery, Family History, Fiction, History, Maritime, Military, Military Classics, Politics, Select, Transport, True Crime, Air World, Frontline Publishing, Leo Cooper, Remember When, Seaforth Publishing, The Praetorian Press, Wharncliffe Local History, Wharncliffe Transport, Wharncliffe True Crime and White Owl.

For a complete list of Pen & Sword titles please contact

PEN & SWORD BOOKS LIMITED
47 Church Street, Barnsley, South Yorkshire, S70 2AS, England
E-mail: enquiries@pen-and-sword.co.uk
Website: www.pen-and-sword.co.uk

Or

PEN AND SWORD BOOKS
1950 Lawrence Rd, Havertown, PA 19083, USA
E-mail: Uspen-and-sword@casematepublishers.com
Website: www.penandswordbooks.com

Table of Contents

Acknowledgements

As with all of my projects, this book would not have been possible without the generous help of many friends. Instrumental to the completion of this book were Dana Bell, Scott Taylor the archivists at the Mack Museum and Rock Island Arsenal, US Army Engineer School History Office, the Ordnance Museum, the members of the National Dusters, Quads and Searchlights Association, the FCA North America Archives, Vintage Power Wagons, David Bundy, David Viscardi, Doug Kibbey, Mike Weaver, Carl T. Heller, Chris Harlow, William Powis, James Lyles, John Adams-Graf, Steve Zaloga, Mike Haines, the staff and volunteers at the Patton Museum, the late Fred Crismon and Eric Mueller, and the staff at the National Archives and TACOM LCMC History Office. Most importantly, I am blessed to have the help and support of my wife Denise, for which I am eternally grateful.

Introduction

The battlefields of Vietnam have been littered with US-built military equipment since World War II. Much of the gear was used by the French during the French-Indochina war, and would be familiar to students of WWII US production. This volume, however, focuses on the vehicles and heavy weapons used by US forces during the period that the United States actively participated in the war in Vietnam from 1965 through 1973.

This book is broken into three major sections, describing wheeled tactical vehicles, track laying combat vehicles, and artillery and heavy weapons, both wheeled and tracked. In all cases, within these groups the topics are arranged by size.

Within these groups, the vehicles are identified by both Standard Nomenclature List (SNL) number, which begins with the letter 'G'. From the mid-1920s until well into the Cold War era, US Army weapons and material were cataloged through a system known as the Standard Nomenclature List (SNL). Within the SNL were various groupings – Group A was automatic weapons, small mortars, carts and light artillery. Group D was heavy field artillery, and most important for the purpose of this book, Group G was tank and automotive material. A numeric suffix was added to the SNL group to define various families of vehicles. For example, the ¾-ton 4 × 4 Dodge truck series which includes the familiar M37 was SNL G-741.

As a rule, the various series of vehicles within each family or numeric suffix have similar power trains and chassis, but the bodies vary – sometimes widely. However, as with so many 'rules', there are a few exceptions to this.

The SNL G system, though not widely used by troops or enthusiasts, is actually much clearer than the more familiar M-number system. In that system, a M1 could be a helmet, a carbine, a rifle, a tank – or a myriad of other things.

Wheeled Vehicles

Quarter-ton trucks – the 'jeeps'

Since World War II, GIs and the public have referred to military ¼-ton 4×4 trucks as jeeps, but in reality, the name 'Jeep' is a trademark which has been owned by a variety of organizations, including Willys-Overland Motors, Kaiser-Willys, American Motors, Kaiser-Jeep and now Fiat-Chrysler. Further, many of the vehicles identified by GIs as jeeps were not only not built by any of these firms, they weren't jeeps at all!

The ¼-ton vehicles used in Vietnam, as a rule, can be broken down into three groups. The first of these is the M38A1/M170 family of vehicles, the SNL G-758 series.

M38A1/M170 SNL G-758

Originally launched in 1949, the M38 was an improved successor of the Jeep that had served in World War II. Unfortunately, however, the vehicle was improved in such a way that its weight increased but its horsepower failed to make up the difference. Accordingly, the M38 had hardly been adopted before work got underway on a better version, dubbed the M38A1. Featuring a new F-head 'Hurricane' power plant, the M38A1 indeed offered greater horsepower than the M38 with its 'Go Devil' L-head engine. Although the new vehicle had begun as a simple revision – hence the 'A1' designation – in fact it evolved into what was practically a totally new vehicle. The Willys firm designated the M38A1 as MD and its civilian model, constructed of comparable sheet-metal and mechanical parts, was the CJ-5.

The M38A1

Willys-Overland Motors in Toledo, Ohio, was the initial manufacturer of the M38A1, beginning in 1952. When Kaiser purchased Willys-Overland on 28 April 1953, the manufacturer's name was changed to Willys Motor Company, a brand that remained unchanged until 1963, when the company was renamed the Kaiser-Jeep Corporation.

Manufacture of the M38A1 continued until 1957. In all, 80,290 vehicles were produced for use in the United States and 21,198 units were made to be sold abroad. Ford of Canada built the M38A1 CDN during the 1950s, while Kaiser-Jeep in Windsor, Ontario, turned out the vehicle during the 1960s.

The M170

A battlefield ambulance version of the G-758 series was produced with the designation M170. The M170's wheelbase was 20 inches longer than that of the M38A1 and the vehicle's internal layout was greatly changed, in keeping with its different purpose. The front seats in this vehicle were narrower, and litter racks were mounted in the rear floor of this ambulance version. Hanging from the bows on the passenger side was an additional litter rack. To provide room for a stretcher, the passenger's seat cushion was removable and could be suspended from the frame of the windshield. A well immediately to the right of the passenger seat accommodated the spare tire and a fuel can. Just behind the driver's seat a droplight on a cable reel was mounted on the left rear wheel well. The back of that seat and its frame pivoted forward and a cushion could be used to latch it to the floor. Mounted in the rear fender wells were storage lockers and numerous special brackets were attached in various locations around the body and tailgate.

A total of 4,155 examples of the M170 were built between 1953 and 1963, most being configured as ambulances. A few of these vehicles, however, were fitted out for use as radio trucks or airfield taxis.

Both the M38A1 and the M170 were used by the US Marine Corps during the early stages of their presence in Vietnam.

GENERAL DATA

MODEL	M38A1	M170
WEIGHT NET GROSS	2690 3865	2963 3763
MAX TOWED LOAD	2000 lbs.	N/A
LENGTH*	138 9/16	155
WHEELBASE*	81	101
WIDTH*	60.625	60.625
HEIGHT*	72.875	80
TIRE SIZE	7.00-16	7.00-16
MAX SPEED	55 mph	55 mph

MODEL	M38A1	M170
FUEL CAPY	13 gallons	13 gallons
RANGE	350 miles	300 miles
ELECTRICAL	24 volt	24 volt
TRANSMISSION SPEEDS	3	3
TRANSFER SPEEDS	2	2
TURNING RADIUS FEET	19.5 R 19 L	24.5 R 24.5 L

* Overall dimensions listed in inches.

ENGINE DATA

ENGINE MAKE/MODEL	Willys MD F-HEAD
NUMBER OF CYLINDERS	4
CUBIC INCH DISPLACEMENT	134
HORSEPOWER	72 @4000
TORQUE	114 @ 2000
GOVERNED SPEED (rpm)	Not Governed

The M38A1 was the first significant change in styling made to the Jeep since the WWII-era MB/GPW were produced. The taller, rounded hood was intended to accommodate the new F-head engine that powered these vehicles. (*TACOM LCMC History Office*)

Production of the M38A1 began in 1952, and the vehicles were initially used by all branches of the US military. This is the M38A1C version, armed with a 106mm recoilless rifle. (*National Archives*)

By the time that the US became heavily involved in Vietnam, the later M151 was the primary ¼-ton vehicle used by the US Army. The Marines, however, continued to rely on the M38A1, as with this 9th Marine Expeditionary Brigade vehicle driving off a ferry at Da Nang on 18 March 1965. (*National Archives*)

USMC M38A1s can be distinguished from their Army siblings in having elongated shackles extending to the side of the rear bumpers, as seen on this example at the Da Nang air field in 1965. (*National Archives*)

At a glance, the M38A1 resembled its civilian sibling, the CJ-5, however the vehicles differed in many ways, not the least of which was the battery box accessible through the lid just in front of the windshield on the passenger's side. The cover for this box can be seen on this M38A1 outside the Combined Action Platoon 3-1 headquarters on 25 August 1967. (*National Archives*)

A variation of the M38A1 was this elongated vehicle, the M170 field ambulance. This example is fully outfitted for deep water fording, with a snorkel for the air intake and an exhaust extension. (*FCA North America Archives*)

The tailgate has been removed from this M170 being displayed by Willys, however the upper litter rack is shown to good advantage, as is the spare tire and ax, both of which were installed in the extended passenger side door opening. (*FCA North America Archives*)

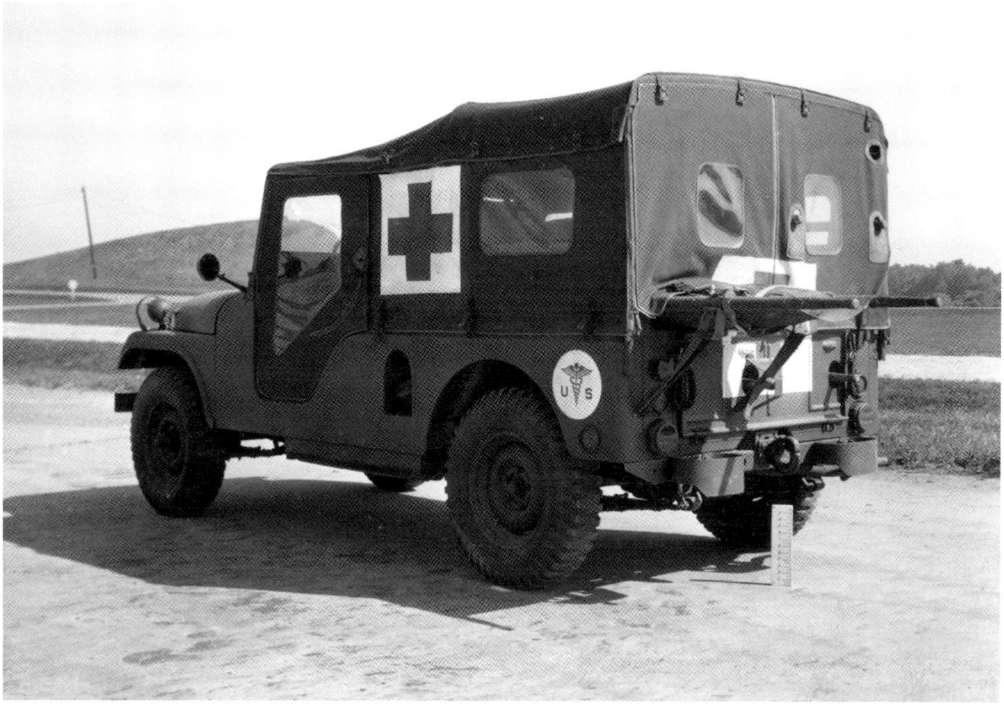

The canvas cover of the M170 carried a red cross on a white field. On the rear of the vehicle half of this symbol was on the canvas, the other half painted on the tailgate. The left-hand litter extended beyond the rear of the M170 body, as seen here. (*National Archives*)

A pad on the rear of the M170 driver's seat protects the head of the left-hand litter patient. The left-hand litter was supported by brackets on the fender-well and the top of the tailgate. There were also two right-hand litters, one resting in floor-mounted brackets, the other suspended from the top bows at the rear. Also visible in this view is the interior-mounted spare tire and a 5-gallon gas can. No bracket for the gas can was installed, but footman's loops were provided to secure it. (*National Archives*)

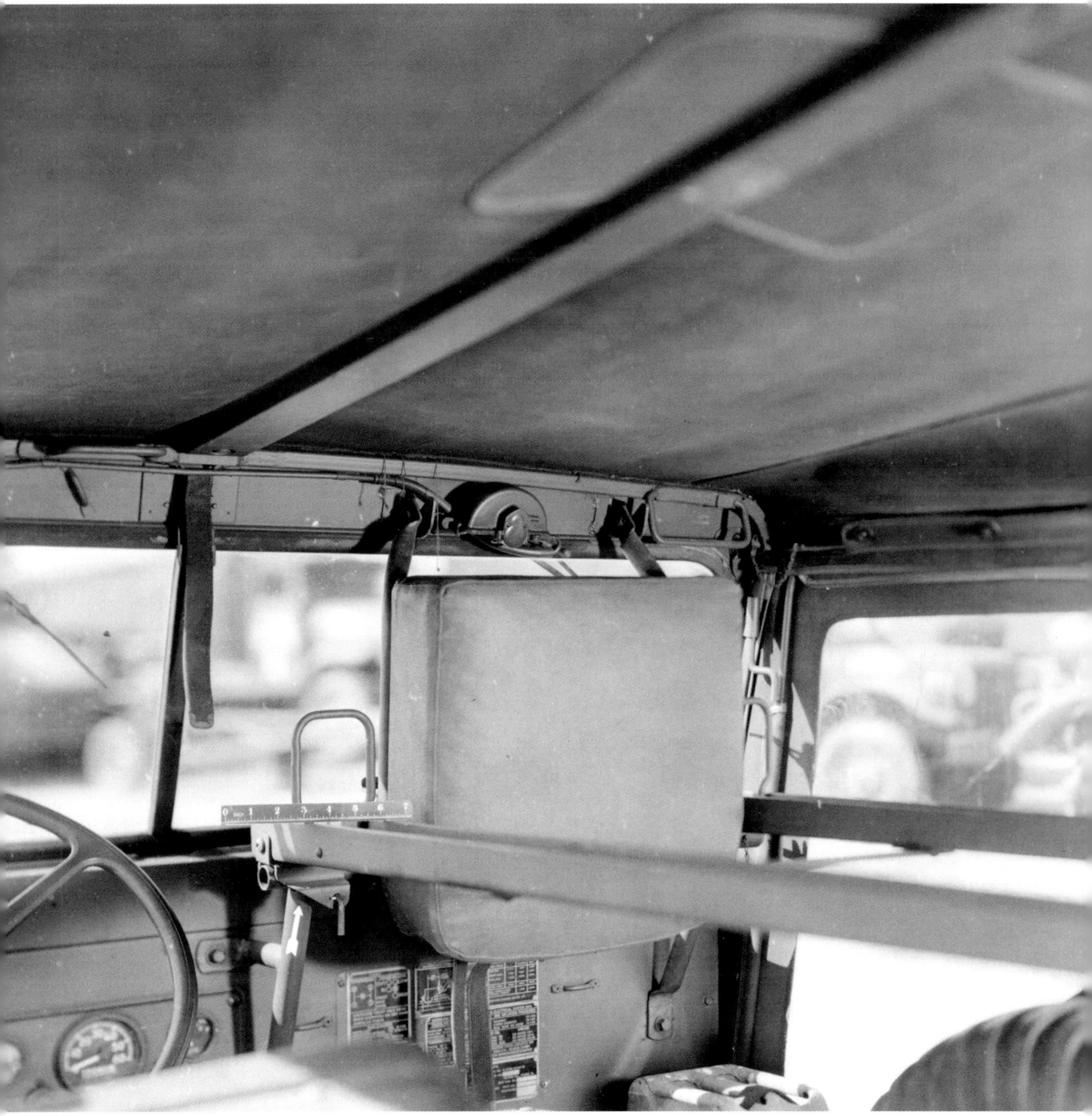

A folding head cushion protected the M170 lower litter patient, while the head of the patient in the upper rack was protected by the repositioned passenger seat cushion. The front of the upper litter rack was supported by a bracket on the dashboard. (*National Archives*)

A M170 was one of the vehicles in this 3rd Battalion, 4th Marines convoy passing through Hue on the way to Phu Bai on 15 April 1965. (*National Archives*)

A M170 passes a Mechanical Mule at a roadblock approaching a bridge secured by bunkers somewhere in Vietnam on 5 October 1965. The Marine Corps style rear bumper is clearly visible in this photo, and can be contrasted with the rear bumper of the Army vehicle seen earlier. (*National Archives*)

M151/M151A1, M718, M151A1C MUTT, SNL G-838

The iconic ¼-ton vehicle of the Vietnam War was the M151-series of trucks. First entering production in 1960, this vehicle, which many GIs refer to as a 'jeep', was in fact not a Jeep at all. Rather, it was designed and initially produced by Ford, which referred to the vehicle as a MUTT (Military Utility Tactical Truck). There were three base models of this vehicle built, the M151, the M151A1 and the M151A2, as well as subvariants, including notably for this volume, a field ambulance.

Nearly nine years after the concept was first broached with Ford, an initial production contract for 4,050 vehicles was awarded on 25 June 1959 under contract number DA-20-018-ORD-21125. Two years later, another contract – DA-20-018-ORD-23240 – was awarded for 13,124 more of the little trucks. Ford set March 1960 as the target date for the delivery of the first of the vehicles covered by the initial contract. Designated M151, these MUTTs were manufactured by Ford at its facility in Livonia, Michigan. In May 1962, Willys Motors secured contract number DA-20-019-ORD-3941 for the manufacture of 14,625 more M151 trucks.

The M151's rear suspension was plagued with problems: in particular, it had a tendency to buckle or collapse, especially under the weight of added cargo or mounted weapons. To overcome this difficulty, the vehicle's rear suspension system was redesigned to include high-strength rear suspension arms with extra bump stops.

In December 1963, Kaiser-Jeep – the new name for Willys Motors, as of March that year – took up manufacture of the M151A1. Just weeks later, on 16 February 1964, Ford received the first multi-year contract (DA-20-113-AMC 02787 [T]) to manufacture the MUTT. Ford was much more interested in this multi-year bid solicitation than it had been in earlier single-year procurement contracts. Nevertheless, Ford placed its bid over objections from the company's car and truck divisions, which feared that this purely military vehicle would overtax their ability to meet civilian market goals. Ford's Industrial Division, accordingly, was given the job of constructing the MUTTs. Ford's Highland Park tractor plant launched the company's manufacture of the M151A1 in the November/December 1964 time frame, and continued producing the vehicles 1969.

Early in the MUTT's career, the Army and other agencies began to raise concerns about the performance of the M151 and M151A1. Accidents started occurring almost immediately after the M151 was introduced. Although the military could blame 'driver error', for each of these mishaps, the frequency of the problems soon made it clear that the performance of the vehicle itself was somehow flawed.

After visiting American troops in Europe, New York Congressman Frank J. Becker – himself a World War I veteran – wrote Defense Secretary Robert S. McNamara (former president of the Ford Motor Company) on 1 November 1961, to relay questions he had encountered from the men in the field regarding the M151's stability.

After two weeks with no response, the Republican Congressman wrote again, this time using language sufficiently forceful to spark an investigation and yet one more redesign of the MUTT. Eventually, these early safety concerns blocked the vehicles from sale on the surplus market at the conclusion of their service after only a handful of units had been released. In the end, the vehicle's handling difficulties would take much longer to resolve than anyone initially would have thought.

The vehicle's fundamental difficulty was that it featured independent suspension. The handling qualities of such a vehicle were quite different from those of all the Army's other tactical vehicles, and different also from anything that soldiers would have encountered in civilian life. To the average driver, the vehicle felt stable when cornering – right up until the actual point that it rolled over. In addition, it was standard practice to test such vehicles with a full load. M151 vehicles were, accordingly, mostly tested when fully laden, in which state they were much less liable to roll over. It was only after the vehicles were fielded that the tendency to roll over appeared.

In fiscal 1967, 3,538 accidents involving the M151 were reported, resulting in 104 deaths and 1,858 injuries. Inattentive drivers were apt to lose control of the vehicle – all too often with fatal consequences – because its rear 'swing-arm' suspension system gave the M151 a lack of body roll when turning and a pronounced oversteer condition. To try to remedy the situation, the Army instituted driver training courses, made films, issued Department of the Army (DA) circulars, and stipulated that no one could drive an M151-series vehicle without obtaining a special endorsement in his or her SF-46 (Driving Permit) allowing for MUTT operation.

Unfortunately, all these measures failed to eliminate the problem and accident reports continued to pile up. The problem with the vehicle needed to be solved, but it was vital to preserve a high level of parts commonality with the M151s and M151A1s that the Army already had in its stocks.

A new rear suspension designed by Ford engineers succeeded in maintaining a degree of parts commonality while also – crucially – addressing the handling problem. The first designation bestowed on this new vehicle was M51A1E1, but this name was soon changed to M151A2. Approval was granted on 25 July 1969 for Limited Production (LP) classification for 24,503 of the redesigned

MUTTs. A number of significant modifications of the M151 series design were incorporated in the new variant. With the hope of reducing the frequency of roll-over accidents, the earlier swing-arm rear suspension was replaced with a semitrailing-arm rear suspension. This suspension system gave the vehicle, even when unloaded, a 'feel' that was more akin to that of a standard automobile when making turns.

However, it appears that none of the M151A2 variants were fielded in Vietnam.

GENERAL DATA

MODEL	M151	M151A1C	M718
WEIGHT NET GROSS	2140 3340	4590	3680
MAX TOWED LOAD	2000 lbs.	2000 lbs.	NA
LENGTH*	132	143.5	143
WIDTH*	62.25	76.5	72
HEIGHT*	71	77.2	76.3
TIRE SIZE	7.00-16	7.00-16	7.00-16
MAX SPEED	66 mph	50 mph	66 mph
FUEL CAPY	17.3	17.3	17.3
RANGE	300 miles	275 miles	300 miles
ELECTRICAL	24 volt	24 volt	24 volt
TRANSMISSION SPEEDS	4	4	4
TRANSFER SPEEDS	1	1	1
TURNING RADIUS FEET	17.9 R 17.8 L	18.5	18.5

* Overall dimensions listed in inches.

ENGINE DATA

NUMBER OF CYLINDERS	4
CUBIC INCH DISPLACEMENT	141.5
HORSEPOWER	71 @ 3800
TORQUE	128 @ 1800

The Ford-designed M151 was the successor to the M38A1 series of ¼-ton trucks. The new design promised better off-road performance, reduced cost and lighter weight. As with most US military vehicles from 1942, the windshield of the M151 would fold down onto the hood, lowering the vehicle's overall height for shipping. The brackets visible below the driver's opening are for stowage of an axe. (*Kevin Emdee collection*)

One of the first ten production vehicles was positioned next to a M38A1 for comparison during evaluation at Fort Knox. The lower body and hood height, as well as overall stance, of the M151 is evident. (*Kevin Emdee collection*)

The M151A1 was an improved model of the M151 featuring a redesigned rear suspension. This M151A1 was produced under Ford's first multi-year production contract for the MUTT, number DA-20-113-AMC 02787 (T), and was photographed while serving as a test vehicle. (*Kevin Emdee collection*)

Sitting in a MUTT, a military policeman works on a report. The vehicle features Chrome-rimmed reddish-orange lights and a reddish-orange siren fitted to the right fender. Some black cushioning appears to be positioned on the bottom of the door opening. (*National Archives*)

Seven M151A1s of the 560th MP Company, 93rd MP Battalion, 16th MP Group, 18th MP Brigade, line up at the 560th's base at Pleiku, South Vietnam, on 10 June 1970. The nearest vehicle displays the motto 'WE AIN'T THE BEST BUT WE'RE DAMN READY' on the side of its cowl. There are machine gun pedestals to the rear of the front seats on the first vehicles. Flashing lights of two different types are visible atop the cowls. (*National Archives*)

Three MUTTs belonging to First Squadron, Ninth Cavalry, First Cavalry Division (Airmobile) head up a convoy driving up Vietnam's Route 1 in July of 1967. Attesting to the ever-present danger of land mines is the GI with a mine detector positioned on the front bumper of the lead vehicle. (*National Archives*)

First Marine Division Leathernecks use an M151A1 MUTT and M416B1 trailer as shields during street battles in Huế, Vietnam, during the Têt Offensive on 5 February 1968. This MUTT features a fording kit often fitted on Marine M151s. On the side of the trailer are a rack and a 5-gallon liquid container. (*National Archives*)

Battery Commander Captain Almarez of G-29th Field Artillery is seen at the entrance to the G-29th compound in Đông Hà, South Vietnam in 1970. A 23-inch Xenon searchlight is fitted on his M151. (*1LT Kevin Leary, G-29th Arty*)

These two M151A1 MUTTs at Đồng Tâm, South Vietnam, in 1969 have been fitted with 23-inch Xenon searchlights. One of the vehicles also features a dash-mounted gun shield. There is a M416 trailer in the background. *(Joel Nelson, 2d Platoon, H-29th Arty)*

MUTTs, like this First Cavalry M151A1, could be equipped with a machine gun fitted on a pedestal mount. Seen in Bình Định Province, South Vietnam, on 22 July 1967, this vehicle has been equipped with an M60 machine gun. The vehicle's sides have also been built up to make room for extra ammunition boxes. *(National Archives)*

Over time, convoys in Vietnam became ever more frequent targets for ambush. Not having any of their own armored vehicles, troops of the 8th Transportation Group responded to the escalating threat of attack by improvising additional armor and equipping their vehicles with automatic weapons. M151s were virtually everywhere in Vietnam and were among the first vehicles to receive such field modification. An example of this kind of upgrade is this example, nicknamed 'Wolfman'. (*US Army Transportation Museum*)

Although the improvised armor plate that was added to the MUTTs was quite thin, it was sufficient to stop a small-arms round, as is attested by this photograph of a Ford-made M151A1, registration number 2G6336. Assembled with hex screws and washers, the additional armor plates were attached to the sides of the vehicle's body. (*MP History Office*)

Besides machine guns, the MUTT could also be modified to carry a mounted M40A1 106mm Recoilless Rifle (RR). Known then as the M151A1C, it was equipped with an M79 mount in which was fitted the recoilless rifle. In turn, atop the RR was an M8C .50-caliber spotting rifle. M151A1C vehicles had a four-man crew and featured single seats for the gunner and loader. To the rear of the vehicle was space for ammunition. (*TACOM LCMC History Office*)

An M151A1C MUTT pauses in a Vietnamese field in the summer of 1970. Armed with a recoilless rifle, this vehicle belongs to a cavalry unit – possibly D-14th Cav. In the background is another MUTT that seems to have elevated rear seating for the M60 machine gunner. Although designed for antitank purposes, recoilless rifles most often saw use in Vietnam as antipersonnel weapons, firing flechette-filled rounds. (*Stan Sohre C-Btry 5/2nd ADA*)

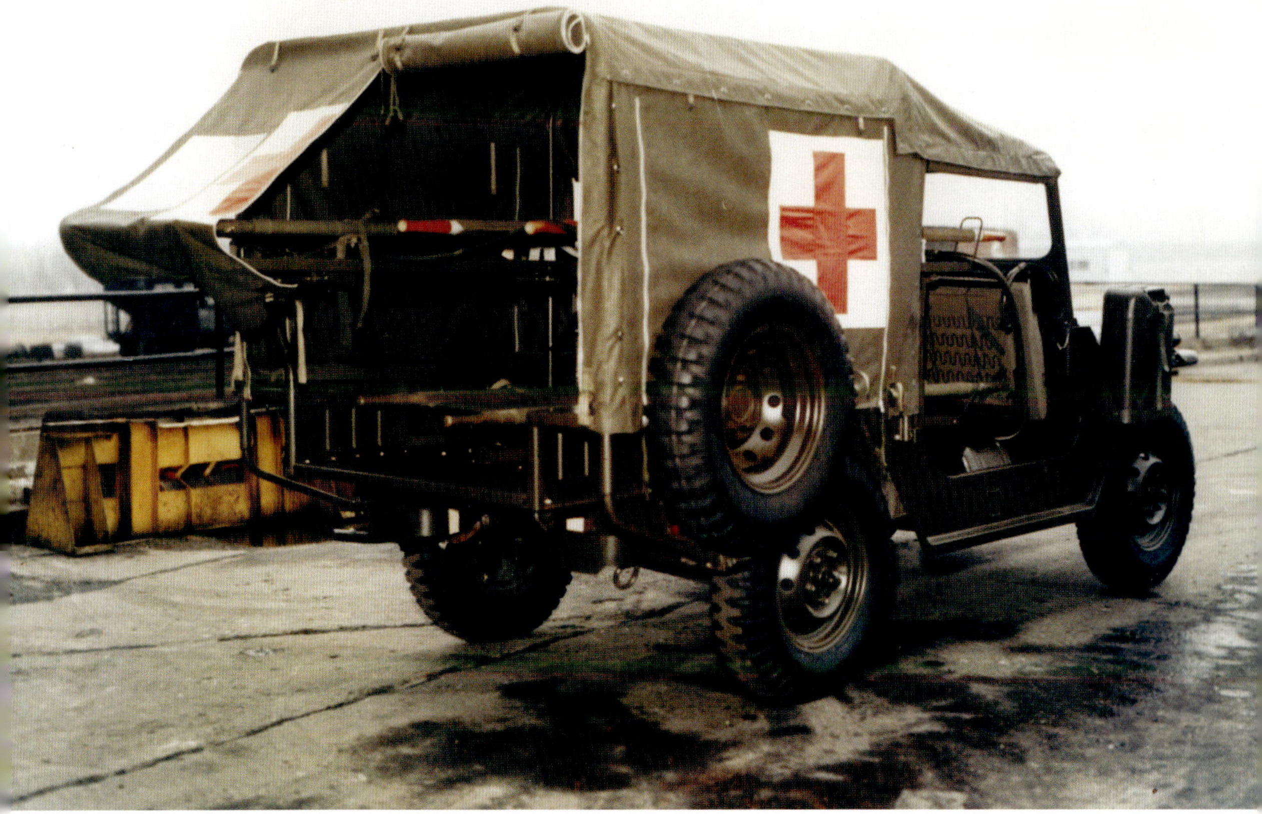

The MUTT's ambulance version, designated the Truck, Ambulance, Front Line, ¼-ton, 4×4, M718, was a development based on the chassis of the M151A1. Entering production in 1966, the M718-family ambulances had room for a driver, a medic, three ambulatory wounded, or two patients in litters plus one ambulatory one. The vehicle could take three litter-borne patients in an emergency. (*TACOM LCMC History Office*)

A medic is seen in the passenger seat of an ambulance MUTT. Stitched onto the vehicle's canvas side-curtain is a red cross made from two cloth rectangles, with the horizontal bar overlapping the vertical one. The bracket for the spare tire is above the mounting eye at the rear of the body. (*Mike Weaver*)

The M422/M422A1 Mighty Mite G-843

A scarce vehicle, but one with a faithful following, was the USMC-specific Mighty Mite. Ben Gregory, a Kansas City-based inventor and former barnstorming pilot, developed the Mighty Mite in 1946–47 and then formed Mid-America Research Corporation (MARCO), in which he received the help of Harold Crist, Ralph Turner, Frank McMillan, and Chet Hemphling – four men who had played key roles in creating the jeep for American Bantam shortly before World War II. Later, as sometimes happens in business, Gregory was forced out of MARCO, despite being the designer who had patented the driveline and suspension of the Mighty Mite.

Prototypes of the Mighty Mite incorporated an imported Porsche engine, but at that time, the US military prohibited use of any imported components, including, of course, that Porsche power plant. Accordingly, the developers had to locate a suitable US-made engine. In the end, American Motors perfected and manufactured the Mighty Mite (before American Motors acquired Jeep) from December 1959 through December 1962.

Featuring an aluminum body and an aluminum engine – the air-cooled 08-cid V-4 – the Mighty Mite weighed in at just less than 1 ton. This low-profile, diminutive, lightweight vehicle that was also highly maneuverable and performed very well in off-road conditions soon drew the attention of the US Marine Corps, which needed a versatile vehicle that would be readily air transportable.

There were two production versions of the Mighty Mite: the M422 and the M422A1. Ten trial M422E1 vehicles were also built. American Motors created the M422E1 by cutting ten of the M422 vehicles in two and lengthening the body and chassis by 6 inches.

Of the original M422 vehicles, only 1,250 were manufactured, but a total of 2,672 of the 6-inch longer M422A1 vehicles were produced. The most visible difference between the two vehicles was the extra 6 inches between the front seat and the rear wheel well. This part of the vehicle also features additional reinforcing embossment in that lengthened area – an additional distinguishing feature. The M422 has a 65-inch wheelbase, while the wheelbase of the M422A1 is 71 inches long.

The Mighty Mites all had four-speed transmission combined with a single-speed transfer case that meant a shorter driveline. With their short turning radius and minimal weight, as well as their limited-slip differentials in front and rear, the Mighty Mites were superb off-road vehicles.

GENERAL DATA

MODEL	M422	M422A1
WEIGHT NET GROSS	1700 2700	1700 2700
MAX TOWED LOAD	1500 lbs.	1500 lbs.
LENGTH*	107	113
WIDTH*	60.625	61
WHEELBASE	65	85
HEIGHT*	59.5	64.5
TIRE SIZE	6.00-16	6.00-16
MAX SPEED	62 mph	62 mph
FUEL CAPY	13 gallons	12 gallons
RANGE	225 miles	225 miles
ELECTRICAL	24 volts	24 volts
TRANSMISSION SPEEDS	4	4
TRANSFER SPEEDS	1	1

* Overall dimensions listed in inches.

ENGINE DATA

ENGINE MAKE/MODEL	American Motors AV-108-4
NUMBER OF CYLINDERS	4
CUBIC INCH DISPLACEMENT	107.8
HORSEPOWER	55 @ 3600
TORQUE	90 @ 2500
GOVERNED SPEED (rpm)	3600

The M422, the initial production Mighty Mite, boasted a short length, tight turning-radius, and, with its aluminum body, was very lightweight. In addition, each of the M422's components was designed to save weight as much as possible. (*TACOM LCMC History Office*)

The most obvious characteristic that distinguished the M422A1 from the earlier M422 was the fact that the distance between the front seat and the rear wheel well of the M422A1 was 6 inches longer than the comparable space on the M422. This elongated area on the M422A1 also featured the added reinforcing embossment that is evident on this newly produced M422A1. This reinforcement also helps distinguish between the two versions of the Mighty Mite. (*FCA North America Archives*)

When the Marines arrived at Da Nang on 12 April 1965, among the vehicles that they used was the M422A1 Mighty Mite. (*National Archives*)

A M422A1 passes beneath a pro-American banner in Hue on its way to Phu Bai on 15 April 1965. These troops are part of 3rd Battalion, 4th Marines. (*National Archives*)

The M422A1 was not originally equipped with a spare tire, but these were often retrofitted in the field. Such is the case with this snorkel-equipped vehicle at Camp Paul C. Evans, 4th Marine Regimental HQ, on 27 June 1967. (*National Archives*)

Additional spare-tire equipped M422A1s are visible in this view of Camp Evans, as well as M416B1 trailers. These trailers were intended for use with the Mighty Mite and are easily distinguished from the common M416 by virtue of the liquid container brackets mounted on each side. (*National Archives*)

A Mighty Mite leaves the Communications Motor Transport area of the First Marine Division, Da Nang, in December 1967. (*National Archives*)

Mule

One of the most unusual vehicles fielded by US forces in Vietnam was the Truck, Platform, Utility, ½ -ton, 4 × 4 – popularly known as the Mechanical Mule. Beginning with a base designation of M274, the vehicle was ultimately fielded in six variants, ending with the M274A5.

While borne from the experimental WWII-era Jungle Burden Carrier, built by Willys-Overland Motors of Toledo, it would be 1953 before the Mule truly began to come into its own, when pilot models of the M274 began to be delivered.

Series production of the type began in 1956, with the M274, but this was soon replaced with the M274A1, which incorporated several minor improvements, most notably the addition of lifting shackles on each wheel hub, an adjustable seat, and incorporation of drum brakes in lieu of the previously used band brakes.

Both the M274 and the M274A1 were powered by the Willys A04-53 four-cylinder engine. The M274A2, built by Bowen McLaughlin-York, was powered by the A042 Military Standard engine two-cylinder engine featuring but a single muffler. This engine proved to be so successful in this application that the earlier M274 and M274A1 models were retrofitted with the two-cylinder engines, becoming M274A3 and M274A4 models respectively.

The M274A5, produced first by Baifield Industries and later by the Brunswick Corporation, differed significantly from previous models, the result of a major redesign. While all the prior models featured four-wheel steering, the M274A5 was two-wheel steering only. The platform deck, which previously had been a magnesium alloy, was now cast of aluminum, as were the axles castings and wheel discs. The vehicle now incorporated a 24-volt electrical system, including starter and headlight, while prior models were recoil start and had no lighting system.

The changes incorporated into the M274A5 were so significant that the vehicle was given its own Standard Nomenclature List (SNL) number – G-400. All previous models were SNL G-823.

While conceived to serve essentially as a small slow-speed truck, the Mule was adapted to carry the 106mm recoilless rifle, and a number of vehicles so-equipped served in Vietnam, alongside their more utilitarian siblings.

GENERAL DATA

MODEL	M274	M274A1	M274A2	M274A3	M274A4	M274A5
WEIGHT NET GROSS	795 1970	900 2075	900 2075		970 1970	
LENGTH*	118.25	119.21	118.25	118.25	119.21	118.25
WHEELBASE*	57	57	57	57	57	57
WIDTH*	49.75	49.75	49.75	49.75	49.75	49.75
HEIGHT*	49.5	49.5	49.5	49.5	49.5	49.5
TIRE SIZE	7.50 x 10	7.50 x 10	7.50 x 10	7.50 x 10	7.50 x 10	7.50 x 10
MAX SPEED	25 mph	25 mph	25 mph	25 mph	25 mph	25 mph
FUEL CAPY	8 gallons	8 gallons	8 gallons	8 gallons	8 gallons	8 gallons
RANGE	107.5	107.5	107.5	107.5	107.5	107.5
ELECTRICAL	NONE	NONE	NONE	NONE	NONE	24 volt
TRANSMISSION SPEEDS	3	3	3	3	3	3
TRANSFER SPEEDS	2	2	2	2	2	2
TURNING RADIUS FEET	10	10	9′ 2″ R 9′ 10″ L	10	10	10

* Overall dimensions listed in inches.

ENGINE DATA

ENGINE MAKE/MODEL	Willys AO-4-53	MIL STD AO42
NUMBER OF CYLINDERS	4	2
CUBIC INCH DISPLACEMENT	53.5	42.4
HORSEPOWER	16 @ 3200	13.5 @ 3000
TORQUE	30 @ 2100	26 @ 2300
GOVERNED SPEED (rpm)	4200	3600

The first production model of the Mechanical Mule was the M274. Known officially as the Truck, Platform Utility, ½-ton, 4×4, the servicemen who used them most often referred to the vehicles merely as the Mule. (*TACOM LCMC History Office*)

The M274 and later M274A1 were powered by a four-cylinder Willys air-cooled engine, and could be distinguished by the two horizontal mufflers, one on each side of the engine, as seen here. (*Ordnance Museum*)

The M274A1 introduced lifting rings on each wheel hub, and the M274A2 utilized a two-cylinder Military Standard engine, rather than the four-cylinder Willys. The two-cylinder engine used only a single muffler, and was later retrofitted to earlier production vehicles, the modified vehicles being designated M274A3 and M274A4. The layout of the two-cylinder engine arrangement is seen on this vehicle being evaluated at Fort Knox. (*Patton Museum*)

The M274A5 was a much different type of Mule, featuring electric start and a headlight, but no longer providing the option of four-wheel steer. This M274A5 was photographed at Aberdeen Proving Ground on 24 November 1967. (*National Archives*)

The Mechanical Mule could also be armed with a 106mm M40 recoilless rifle, as is this USMC example going ashore at Da Nang on 8 March 1965. (*National Archives*)

The 184th Ordnance Battalion was using the Mechanical Mule, in this instance driven by Pfc Weise, to deliver 105mm howitzer ammunition near Qui Nhon, on 26 August 1966. Despite its small stature, the Mule had a greater cargo capacity than the jeep. (*National Archives*)

Marines of the 9th Marine Regiment stack cases of rations on a Mule near Khe Sanh on 22 April 1968. In the background a Mighty Mite passes by. The low profile of the Mule is clearly evident when compared to the Marines loading it. That low profile, four-wheel drive and high load to weight ratio made the vehicle well suited for supply missions in hostile areas. (*National Archives*)

At Phu Tai, SP4 Tom Dormer unloads a 19th Supply and Service Company Mule on 8 June 1970. From the position of the wheels, it appears that the four-wheel steer of this two-cylinder engine powered vehicle is enabled. (*National Archives*)

Dodge ¾-ton 4 × 4 M37 family G-741 series

The ¾-ton 4 × 4 truck served as essentially the US military's 'pickup truck' during the Vietnam War. The truck was small enough to be reasonably maneuverable in towns and camps, yet robust enough to negotiate muddy and rugged terrain. Its cargo/troop capacity was adequate for the intended task.

M37

During WWII and Korea, Dodge-built vehicles dominated the US military's ¾-ton 4 × 4 vehicle fleet. Not surprisingly, when the Army began looking for a ¾-ton truck, featuring the refinements standard across the post-WWII vehicle line – 24-volt electrical system, integral deep-water fording, standardized components across the whole tactical vehicle fleet – the Army again turned to Chrysler's Dodge division.

Chrysler received a government request dated 4 October 1948 for a formal quotation for such a new type of truck. Detroit Arsenal gave Chrysler five weeks (i.e., until 8 November) to provide pricing for 1,600, 2,000, 2,250, and 2,500 of such trucks. That vehicle would be the M37, and the series was given Standard Nomenclature List number G-741.

On 14 December 1950, the first production pilot of the M37 serial number 80006010 was finished. (The production pilot is, of course, distinct from six earlier pre-production pilot vehicles.) These G-741 trucks would continue to be manufactured until serial number 80264200 on 2 July 1954. The tooling for the vehicle was then put into storage. Within a few years, the Army felt a need for more of the trucks and on 27 June 1957, a contract for 3,400 more G-741 vehicles was issued. Dodge took the tooling out of storage and, after making a few minor design changes, prepared to restart manufacture of the vehicle, now designated M37B1. The deadline for the completion of the new trucks was set at 30 June 1958.

The M37B1 vehicles received an improved New Process Model 420 transmission. The Douglas connectors – metal twist-lock connections – that were used on G-741 trucks were replaced by rubber-enclosed Packard connectors. Another change on the M37B1 was that the spare tire, which had been located in the bed, was now moved to a position outside the driver's door, where it was mounted on a swing-out spare-tire carrier of the sort previously designed for the M43 Ambulance. Except for 1960 and 1966, the M37B1 would remain in production into 1968.

V41

Built on an M56 chassis, the V41 featured a telephone maintenance and installation body specified by the Armed Services Electro Standards Agency, Ft. Monmouth, New Jersey. The trucks were also fitted with a Braden LU-4 front-mounted PTO-driven winch with a 7,500-pound capacity. The truck bed had a low tailgate and a center aisle, and on either side were four storage compartments that opened outward. In addition, the open top bed was the location of the spare tire, carried internally. Above the bed was a ladder rack and on the driver's side was a water cooler. For night operation, a spotlight was mounted near the driver's door. Production of the V41/GT was initially contracted for in June 1951, and its specification, MIL-T-10158B, was last updated on June 30, 1957. Ultimately, a total of 599 of these trucks were built. Officials started to call the telephone line maintenance truck the XM201 rather than the V41.

The Detroit Ordnance District on 20 March 1959 asked Chrysler for a proposal on the manufacture of 2,500 G-741 trucks with the B1 improvements. These vehicles had to be delivered between May 1959 and March 1960. The request specifically asked for 309 winch-equipped M201B1 vehicles. Chrysler records relating to these trucks carry the notation: 'The latter differed in a number of details from the ¾-ton V41 Telephone Maintenance Trucks last built by the Dodge Truck Plant under Contract No. 12107 in 1953.' A total of 521 of the M201B1 trucks were delivered between 1960 and 1963.

M43 Ambulance

Two variations of ambulance form part of the G-741 series vehicles: the M43, which was initially contracted for in May 1950, and the M43B1, which was first ordered in March 1958.

All of these ambulances featured a swing out spare tire carrier which was mounted outboard of the driver's door. This type of spare tire carrier was also used throughout the B1 series of trucks, regardless of body type.

The Detroit Ordnance District requested a proposal for more G-741 vehicles on 18 March 1958. Included were 300 M43B1 ambulances with Red Cross markings and 60 M43B1 with plain olive drab paint. On contract DA-20-018-AMC-1175(T) another 560 M43B1 ambulances were ordered in 1964.

XM708 ¾-ton Dump Truck

Specifications for the XM708 were laid down by MIL-T-62114(AT) on 8 May 1969. This ¾-ton dump truck was based on the M53B1 chassis (not, as is widely thought, on the M56 chassis). The M708 shared the 12-inch wheelbase and driveline with the M37, but it came without a bed. The M56 chassis, which was similar, had a 126-inch wheelbase and served as the foundation for other Dodge variants.

The SC-2300-IL of July 1969 indicates that three varieties of the XM708 were manufactured. These varieties were as follows:

- Dump Truck XM708 with Gar Wood dump body, FSN 2320-911-5071, acquisition cost $6,202.00.
- Dump Truck XM708E1 with Hardeman dump body FSN 2320-911-5078, acquisition cost $6,202.00.
- Dump Truck XM708 with winch and Gar Wood dump body. These units have a Federal Stock Number of 2320-926-7154, and although a winch has been added to the vehicle, the unit cost is only $6,150.00.

The cost figures cited above do not include the M53B1 chassis, which the US government furnished to the dump body vendor. This fact helps account for the lower cost of the trucks that are equipped with winches, since they already came with a PTO that would have been added to the others.

These dump trucks could double as troop transports, since their dump beds were specifically designed to accommodate the standard troop seats and bows found on the M37B1 Cargo Truck.

XM711 Wrecker

Like the dump trucks in the XM708 series, the XM711 Wreckers were constructed on the special M53B1 chassis. MS51390A, the chassis specification, carries the date of 9 June 1967. The specification for the XM711 itself (Military Specification MIL-T-62115) carries a 13 May 1969 date.

A requirement of this specification was that all chassis used in XM711 manufacture come equipped with a power takeoff-driven front-mounted winch. In accordance with that requirement, and according to the Supply Catalogue 2300-IL of July 1969, all XM711 wrecker trucks came with the Braden LU-4 front winch, which had a 7,500-pound capacity. To prepare them for use in wrecker trucks, the chassis were fitted with strengthened front springs and also, at the rear, overload, similar to those on the XM708.

Manually operated wrecker beds were featured on the XM711. These beds, the Ashton model 10-60BW, were produced by the Ashton Equipment Company.

Mounted just behind the cab was a power takeoff-driven rear winch, made by Tulsa. That winch had a rated single-line pull of 30,000 pounds on bare drum, and its load capacity was 12,000 pounds. Wound on the winch drum and woven up the boom of the wrecker was a wire rope with a 7/16-inch diameter and length of 250 feet. The wrecker boom was telescopic; it was 90 inches long when retracted and 138 inch inches in length when extended. In the normal towing position, the boom had a rated capacity of 3½ tons. When fully extended, the boom's capacity was 800 pounds. Control levers, mounted at the rear of the bed, allowed operators to control the wrecker operation using a series of linkages, just as was the case on Ashton's commercial units.

GENERAL DATA

MODEL	M37	M42	M43	V41/GT-M201	CMU-3
WEIGHT NET GROSS	5687 7687	6050 7550	7150 8550	6950 9300	
MAX TOWED LOAD	4000	4000	N/A	6000	
LENGTH*	184.75	184.75	195.625	203.75	
WHEELBASE*	112	112	126	126	126
WIDTH*	73.5	73.5	73.5	73.5	73.5
HEIGHT*	89.5	89.75	91.875	92.75	89.5
TRACK	62	62	62	62	62
TIRE SIZE	9.00-16	9.00-16	9.00-16	9.00-16	9.00-16
MAX SPEED	55 mph	55 mph	55 mph	55 mph	55 mph
FUEL CAPY	24 gallons	24 gallons	24 gallons	24 gallons	24 gallons
RANGE	215 miles	215 miles	215 miles	215 miles	215 miles
ELECTRICAL	24 negative	24 negative	24 negative	24 negative	24 negative
TRANSMISSION SPEEDS	4	4	4	4	4
TRANSFER SPEEDS	2	2	2	2	2
TURNING RADIUS FEET	25	25	27	25	25

* Overall dimensions listed in inches.

All information above is for vehicle without winch (where applicable). For winch-equipped vehicles, add 230 pounds to weights listed, and increase length 4⅝ inches.

ENGINE DATA

ENGINE MAKE/MODEL	Dodge T245
NUMBER OF CYLINDERS	6
CUBIC INCH DISPLACEMENT	230.2
HORSEPOWER	78 @3200
TORQUE	177 @ 1200
GOVERNED SPEED (rpm)	3200

In July 1948, Chrysler designed a new model of the ¾-ton 4x4 truck in conjunction with the Detroit Arsenal. Designated the M37 by the Ordnance Department, this and other trucks sharing common components would become staples of US military motor pools through the middle of the 1970s. A Dodge M37 that looks fresh from the factory bears USA number 201009578 and is seen here from the left side. The running boards that were found on both sides of the M37 cab were topped by a nonslip tread. *(Vintage Power Wagons collection)*

It had been almost four years since Dodge had ended production of its M37 when, in 1958, the Dodge M37B1 Cargo Truck made its appearance. Although very similar to the M37, the M37B1 incorporated a few distinguishing differences. The M37B1's spare tire was mounted outside the driver's door on a pivoting carrier that could be unlocked from inside or outside the truck. To allow for the door to open, the carrier would be swung out of the way. The transmission and electrical system of the M37B1 were also improved over those on the M37. M37B1, USA. number 3B5812, is seen here at a Chrysler plant in Detroit on 11 May 1961. (*Vintage Power Wagons collection*)

A Dodge M37B1 plows through the muck on a road in an ammunition dump at Fire Support Base Bronco in South Vietnam during the Cambodian incursion on 22 June 1970. The driver's door, the spare-tire carrier, and the windshield have been removed from the truck. (*National Archives*)

Assigned to the 266th Supply and Service Battalion, 29th Support Group, 11th Armored Cavalry Regiment, this Dodge M37B1 pulls an M101 trailer up the road from Long Binh to Fire Support Base Holiday Inn near Biên Hòa, South Vietnam, in late December 1968. (*National Archives*)

Communicating with loved ones back in the States was complicated and slow for servicemen in the Vietnam War. In that now forgotten age before cell phones and the Internet, one way troops could reach out to friends and family was by putting a call through the Military Affiliate Radio System (MARS) in which stations at selected places in the United States were manned by ham radio operators who would relay the call. Mobile MARS Station No. 1 is seen here at Xuân Lộc, near Saigon, South Vietnam, on 20 April 1971. The station features an S-318 shelter on a Dodge M37B1 truck with the USA. number 3C5024. (*National Archives*)

The V41 ¾-ton 4×4 Telephone Maintenance Truck was one of the three truck models envisaged in the initial G-741-series contract, the other models being the M37 Cargo Truck and M42 Command Truck. The V41 featured a soft cab top, a Braden LU4 winch with a 7,500-pound capacity, and an all-steel service body. There were parts, tool cabinets, and racks above the body for an extension ladder and lineman's poles. The intended users of the V41 were Signal Corps crews who installed, maintained, and spliced telephone lines. (*Vintage Power Wagons collection*)

Included in the second US Army contract for Dodge G-741/Model T245 trucks was a field ambulance version. This vehicle, designated the M43, ultimately served in Vietnam. A spotlight was mounted atop the cab of the M43, which was based on the M56 chassis with a 126-inch wheelbase. (*Vintage Power Wagons collection*)

Near the left rear wheel well of the M43 was an oval-shaped recess in which were located the fuel filler and cap. To the front of the rear wheel well was a door to a stowage compartment. The spare tire was mounted on a pivoting carrier by the driver's door. To allow the driver to get in and out through the left door, the spare tire carrier could be swung aside.

Parked at the rear of a CH-47 helicopter is a Dodge M43B1 field ambulance, USA. number 3B5980, taking part in the medical evacuation of a wounded soldier during the search-and-destroy mission code named Operation Junction City, Phase II, on 6 April 1967. White stenciling that appears to be in Vietnamese is visible to the rear of the vehicle's red cross. (*National Archives*)

The original purpose of the CMU-3 Contact Maintenance Truck was to carry out roadside repairs and maintenance on tactical, combat, and engineer vehicles. This truck was based on a Dodge chassis with a 126-inch wheelbase, and there is documentary evidence indicating that this was the M56C chassis. There is, however, other documentation that points to the M56B1 chassis being the basis for some CMU-3s. While the CMU-3 body was of steel, the similar CMU-5 had an aluminum body. Here an Army Engineer field contact team stand by with their CMU-3 truck, its left-hand service doors hanging open. In the front compartment of the truck, whose USA number is 3A6165, is the generator-welder's control panel. At the upper left of the control panel is a large, round feature – the ten-range switch – that the operator used to select the desired welding amperage. Also included on the panel are an AC and DC voltmeter, a DC ammeter, a welder polarity control, a control for engine starting, and other controls and switches. There is a welder's hood in the center compartment, and there are tools and kits in the upper rear compartment. (*Patton Museum*)

A limited number of dump trucks were produced as part of the G-741 ¾-ton 4x4 series. Three models of the vehicles were delivered: the XM708 with a Gar Wood GA-2 dump body; the XM708E1 with the Hardeman dump body; and the XM708 with the Gar Wood GA-2 dump body and a winch. (*Vintage Power Wagons collection*)

A G-741 Dodge Dump Truck plows through mud at a base camp in Vietnam. Unit markings on the truck's bumper identify it as belonging to A Company, 15th Engineer Battalion, 9th Infantry Division. The 15th Engineer battalion left Vietnam headed to Hawaii in August 1969. The truck's dump body has three bows and lazy backs installed on it. (*David Viscardi*)

Three XM708 Dump Trucks, are seen among other vehicles in a Vietnamese field. Each of the XM708s is hitched to a trailer covered with a tarpaulin. (*David Bundy*)

Another member of the G-741 family of Dodge vehicles was the XM711 wrecker. Based on an M53B1 chassis with a 126-inch wheelbase, the XM711 featured a Braden LU-4 front winch and a spare tire carrier on its left side. The truck was equipped with a model 10-60-BW commercial telescoping boom made by the Ashton Power Wrecker Equipment Company. (*Vintage Power Wagons collection*)

The 2½-ton 6 × 6

The 2½-ton 6 × 6 was the backbone of the US military tactical vehicle fleet from World War II well into the Vietnam War. The trucks were rated with 2½-ton cross country load capacity, which could be doubled when operating on improved roads. In practice, both of these rated capacities were often well exceeded. The 2½-ton chassis was used as the basis for numerous specialized vehicle configurations, including repair shops, communications bases, water purification, signals maintenance, fire fighting and many others. The base vehicles served as cargo and troop carriers, although in time the similar-looking 5-ton 6 × 6 began to overshadow the 2½-ton truck in the cargo and dump roles.

Two families of 2½-ton 6 × 6 trucks were used in Vietnam, although one, the Hydramatic transmission-equipped GMC was only used in country for a very brief period of time.

M135/M211 GMC G-749 SERIES TRUCKS

After the end of the Second World War, GMC hoped to continue to dominate the market for tactical trucks that the company had established with the CCKW. So when Reo Motors' G-742 took center stage as the main tactical cargo truck, GMC refused to give up, offering its own truck as an alternative to the government. This alternative was the innovative M135 (G-749) truck series that GMC developed in 1951. These vehicles were equipped with automatic transmissions, air-assisted power brakes, and oversized single tires. As it turned out, the M135 would remain only a secondary truck in US service, but it would become the standard truck in use by Canadian forces for many years.

The GMC 302 straight six-cylinder gasoline engine powered all the M135 trucks. The series' initial transmission – GMC's 302M Hydramatic – was soon replaced with the improved 303M, which like its predecessor featured four forward and one reverse speed in either of two ranges. These transmissions also featured a rear pump that allowed the truck to be push-started in emergency situations – an uncommon feature in automatic transmissions. The two-range transmission meant that a single-speed transfer case was used.

The M135's axles were also designed by GM. A dog-type clutch facilitated front-axle engagement whenever the rear wheels slipped. No manual selection for all-wheel drive was provided. Service brakes were of an air over hydraulic power-assisted design. The service brake system on all production vehicles in the M135 series had built-in electric parking brakes in addition to the normal drum-type parking brakes. None of the M135s featured power steering.

When trucks were equipped with winches, the model used was the Gar Wood CA514 10,000-pound winch that had been fitted to trucks in the G-742 series. The mounting brackets and the winch drive line were, however, different from those on the G-742 vehicles. Somewhat unusually for military trucks, the M135s had the same overall length, regardless whether they were fitted with a winch or not. Distinctive lightening holes were a feature of the vehicles' front bumper, which was inverted to allow for cable clearance on these trucks. Inside the cab were mounted pioneer tools. On the driver's side step was mounted an auxiliary fuel container, i.e., a Jerry can.

The number of these trucks that actually saw service in Vietnam was small, and those were only in country during the early period of direct American involvement in the conflict.

M135 Cargo Truck

Entering production in September 1951, the M135 Cargo Truck was the first vehicle in the series. Fitted with six 11.00-20 tires, these trucks had a cargo bed with wheel wells that allowed for lower mounting to make it easier for troops to enter and deploy from the vehicle. A fold-out step on the tailgate of the early trucks also facilitated entrance and egress. The vehicle's bed was slightly narrower than that of dual-wheel trucks. As a result, bows, supports, and canvas covers could not be interchanged with those of dual-wheel vehicles.

M211 and XM211 Cargo truck

The second vehicle in series, the M211 and XM211 had the same 156-inch wheelbase as the M135, but was fitted with 10 9.00-20 tires. Less of a general purpose vehicle than the M135, these trucks were intended mainly for use as on-road cargo transports. Their beds had flat floors (no wheel wells) and were mounted higher than the beds on the M135 trucks. The fold-out tailgate step found on the M135 was absent from the M211 and XM211 tailgate, which had only simple hoop steps such as were featured on most 6 × 6s.

	M135	M211
WEIGHT ^	12,330	13,170
LENGTH*	269	269
WIDTH*	88	96
HEIGHT*	105	112
TIRE SIZES	11.00-20	9.00-20
MAX SPEED	58 mph	55 mph
FUEL CAPY	56 GAL	56 GAL
RANGE	300 Miles	300 Miles

^ without winch, winch equipped vehicles are 410 pounds heavier.
* Overall dimensions listed in inches.

When introduced in 1951, the M135 was a very innovative vehicle compared to the WWII-era CCKW. Boasting six 11.00-20 tires rather than dual rear wheels, the truck had superior off road mobility. This was further enhanced by the incorporation of an automatic transmission. (*TACOM LCMC History Office*)

The M135 was not widely used in Vietnam, however, when the 173rd Airborne Brigade arrived in country, they brought their GMCs with them. Here 173rd troopers clamber on a M135 near the Bien Hoa and Vung Tau airfields on 5 May 1965. (*National Archives*)

Whereas the M135 excelled at off-road performance, the M211 was developed to provide improved on-road performance as well as ease of cargo handling. Although equipped with 9.00-20 tires, with duals in the rear, and a bed which lacked wheel wells, mechanically it was identical to the M211. (*TACOM LCMC History Office*)

Here members of the 1st Cavalry Division (Airmobile) unload from a M211 to board a C-130 at Nha Trang on 25 August 1965. Like the M135, the M211 was rarely used in Vietnam. (*National Archives*)

The M35 family of 2½-ton trucks, the G-742 series

The dual-wheeled M35 was a derivative of the M34 that rode on six 11.00-20 tires. Reo Motors, Inc., based in Lansing, Michigan, designed the M34, and in 1949, pilot models of the vehicle were subjected to testing.

Superior off-road performance was provided by single 11.00-20 tires. For off-road operation, however, dual-wheels were preferred, and the M35 was therefore fitted with dual rear wheels. Using slightly smaller 9.00-20 tires allowed the truck bed to be flat, by eliminating the wheel wells. A straight, flat bed made loading the truck much easier. Both the M34 and M35 had a 154-inch wheelbase.

After war broke out in Korea in 1950, a major concern for strategic planners in the United States was the possibility of the conflict escalating into World War III. Worry over such a scenario prompted the development of new strategic industrial plans to facilitate a major arms buildup.

There was concern that Reo Motors had insufficient industrial capacity to be able to satisfy the military's demand for the new 2½-ton truck, particularly with the possibility of global war looming on the horizon. Studebaker, based in South Bend, Indiana, was grappling with financial difficulties in 1950, and by awarding a contract to that company to produce additional 2½-ton trucks, the military secured an adequate supply of trucks while the economic welfare of Studebaker and the US economy as a whole were given a shot in the arm. Accordingly, in 1950, just months after Reo received its 2½-ton truck contract in June 1949, Studebaker got a 2½-ton truck contract.

The family of vehicles designated G-742 in the US army's Standard Nomenclature List included both the M34 and M35 2½-ton cargo. About 101,000 gasoline-engine G-742 trucks were manufactured in a variety of body types: cargo truck, tanker, van, and numerous other specialized bodies.

For a long time the US Military sought an engine that was able to burn multiple fuels. If an engine could burn gasoline, diesel, jet fuel, or some blend of these, great advantages would accrue from the standpoint of the supply chain and from the standpoint of simply being able to make use of whatever sort of combustible was readily available in any given theater of operations.

In answer to this need, Continental Motors redesigned its TD-427 six-cylinder truck powerplant into the multifuel LDS-427 engine. The military contracted to receive twenty-two test trucks of the M35E7 type incorporating the new multifuel powerplant.

The engine used in those twenty-two trucks was, to be specific, a straight-six LDS-427-2 Multifuel powerplant that had displacement of 427 cubic inches. These engines could – without any adjustment or modification – burn diesel, jet fuel, kerosene, gasoline, or any combination of those various fuels. Following exhaustive trials, this powerplant was adopted and incorporated into the series G-742 trucks. The G-742 cargo truck version that was equipped with this engine received the designation M35A1. Introduced in June 1963, this vehicle had a horizontal exhaust pipe that exited over the tandem axles on the right side – the same configuration as that found on the gasoline-powered version of the truck.

A total of 16,070 trucks were manufactured using the LDS-427-2 engine. In June 1965, that engine was replaced by the LD-465 series of Multifuel powerplants, which had a slightly larger displacement (478 cubic inches) and was more robust. Cargo trucks incorporating this engine received the designation M35A2.

Naturally aspirated, these engines featured an exhaust that exited over the right-side tandems just like the configuration on previous trucks. When the LD-465-1C engine was introduced in later production trucks, a vertical exhaust made its appearance. On these vehicles the exhaust flowed from the powerplant to the muffler underneath the cab and then went forward and up a vertical exhaust pipe with a 2½- inch diameter that extended through the rear of the front fender on the vehicle's right side. In all, some 125,000 trucks were constructed with this powerplant.

Just prior to the withdrawal of US combat forces from Vietnam, the turbo-supercharged LDT-465-1C replaced the LD-465-1C. The purpose of the turbosupercharger was not to increase horsepower, but instead was introduced to comply with restrictions instituted by the Environmental Protection Agency (EPA). When the older engines wore out, LDT powerplants were installed in their place. Later, in turn, the LDT-465-1D replaced the LDT-465-1C. Trucks equipped with the LDT-465 powerplant also had a vertical exhaust pipe – one with a diameter of 3½ inches – but since the system had no muffler, the pipe merely turned up vertically underneath the vehicle's right front fender and then exited that fender through a hole.

G-742 GENERAL DATA

MODEL	**154″ wheelbase cargo trucks**	**190″ wheelbase cargo trucks**	**154″ wheelbase van trucks**	**190″ wheelbase van trucks**
WEIGHT NET^	12465	13500	15231	20609
WEIGHT GROSS^	23230	23500	20581	25959
MAX TOWED LOAD	10000	10000	10000	10000
LENGTH*^	262	324	263	324
WIDTH*	96	96	969	96
HEIGHT*	112	124.5	130	132
WHEELBASE*	154	190	154	190
TIRE SIZE	9.00 – 20	11.00 – 20	9.00 – 20	9.00 – 20
MAX SPEED	58	58	58	58
FUEL CAPY	50	50	50	50
RANGE LOADED	300	300	300	300
ELECTRICAL	24 Neg	24 Neg	24 Neg	24 Neg
TRANSFER SPEEDS	2	2	2	2
TRANSMISSION SPEEDS	5 F	5 F	5 F	5 F
TURNING RADIUS FEET	35.5	45	35.5	35.5

All data given above are for gas powered, dual wheel trucks where available, for other powerplants please adjust as shown below. Data given for trucks less winch, except wreckers which all had front winches.

* Overall dimensions listed in inches.
^ Add 650 lbs to weight on vehicles powered by the Multifuel engine.
^ Add approximately 500 lbs to weight and 14' to length for front winch.

ENGINE DATA

ENGINE MAKE/MODEL	Reo OA-331	LDS-427	LD-465
NUMBER OF CYLINDERS	6	6	6
CUBIC INCH DISPLACEMENT	331	427	478
HORSEPOWER	146 @ 3400	140 @ 2600 RPM	130
TORQUE	330	180 @ 1800 RPM	305 @ 2000

The truck that would become the iconic US 6x6 from the 1950s through the 1980s was designed by Reo Motors of Lansing, Michigan. In its earliest form, the M34, seen in this 1949 photo, the truck originally rode on six 11.00-20 tires. The M34, produced by both Reo and Studebaker into the mid-1950s, had largely been withdrawn from front-line service prior to large numbers of US troops being committed to Vietnam. *(TACOM LCMC History Office)*

In an effort to improve cargo handling, the M35 was introduced. Rather than six 11.00-20 tires, the M35 used ten 9.00-20 tires with duals on the rear. The M35 also dispensed with the wheel wells in the cargo bed, creating a flat loading floor, at the price of a slight decrease in off-road performance. Like the M34, Reo and Studebaker and Studebaker's successor companies built the M35. (*TACOM LCMC History Office*)

M35s and five-ton dump trucks of the 1st Battalion, 18th Infantry, 1st Infantry Division, roll along the beach at Cam Rahn Bay on 12 July 1965. The right-side engine compartment side-panel is open on the winch-equipped M35 in the foreground. Notably, the windshield of both M35s has been folded onto the hoods. (*National Archives*)

While the wheel-well-less bed of the M35 family of vehicles did make cargo stowage easier as a result of not having to position cargo around the protruding wheel wells, it was still far from ideal. As early as 1953 the Army began experimenting with a drop-side cargo body, as seen here, which would allow forklift loading of pallets into the truck. (*TACOM LCMC History Office*)

The USMC became the first user of the drop-side version the trucks, including this example photographed fording the An Long River, 20 miles north of the Landing Zone Tombstone, in January 1968. (*National Archives*)

Since WWII, the US Army had desired that its tactical vehicles be able to operate on gasoline, Diesel fuel and a range of other combustibles, without modification. This led to Continental developing their Multifuel engine. The first production model 2½-ton truck powered by the Multifuel-powered cargo truck was the M35A1. The right-side engine compartment panel was altered to accommodate the mushroom-shaped air intake. The exhaust was above the right-side tandems; in the same location it had been on the base M35 truck.

A Multifuel cargo truck is part of a 9th Infantry Division convoy rolling through the Cholon section of Saigon on 26 July 1969. Further back in the convoy a 2½-ton truck is laden with a pair of M105 trailers. (*National Archives*)

The LDS-427 Multifuel which powered the M35A1 was somewhat trouble-prone, and it was soon supplanted by the LD-465 Multifuel engine. With the change of engine came a change of the truck designation, the basic cargo truck becoming the M35A2, as seen here being lifted into the hold of the *Wayne Victory* as the 9th Infantry Division was withdrawn from Vietnam in July 1969. (*National Archives*)

This pair of 1966 Kaiser-Jeep M35A2 trucks, assigned to G-Battery, 65th Artillery Quads, are powered by LD-465 naturally aspirated Multifuel engines, the exhaust outlets for which are visible above the rear tandems. The quad mounts in the back of the trucks, originally intended for antiaircraft defense, are probably being used for perimeter defense at this firebase in I Corps Tactical Zone. (*National Archives*)

Gun trucks of the 572nd Transportation Company, US Army, with Marines aboard prepare for a convoy mission in April 1968. The nearest vehicle is a 1966 Kaiser-Jeep M35A2. The second truck in line is 'Kong Killer'. In the background is a 2½-ton truck with a quad .50-caliber machine gun mount and partially hidden in the background is a M42 Duster self-propelled antiaircraft gun, armed with two 40mm Bofors automatic guns. This group of vehicles is likely preparing for convoy escort. (*National Archives*)

Later M35A2s, such as this one, featured a vertical exhaust stack. Soon thereafter a stone shield made of expanded metal, attached to the grille to further protect the radiator, was added, as seen here. The later trucks also had notably larger NATO-style taillights and turn signals. (*National Archives*)

Counter to popular belief, a few of these later style M35A2 trucks did see service in Vietnam, as evidenced by this photo of one such truck involved in the construction of a berm line at Fire Support Base Lynch, Long Kahn Province in July 1970. (*National Archives*)

190″ wheelbase cargo trucks

As previously mentioned, the M34/M35/M35A1/M35A2 all were 154-inch wheelbase trucks intended to transport cargo or personnel. These trucks were designated by the military as 'long wheel base' trucks (as opposed to the 142-inch wheelbase configuration used by tractor-trucks and some dump trucks). The G-742 series of trucks also included a 'extra-long wheelbase' chassis with a 190-inch wheelbase, some of which were used for cargo trucks. The M36 was the first of the vehicles in this extra long wheel base series. Like the long wheelbase trucks, the first models were powered by the OA-331 gasoline engine, and the truck evolved through the LDS-427 and LD-465 powerplants as well. Regardless of engine, all these trucks were equipped with dual 9.00-20 rear wheels. These trucks were dedicated cargo carriers, and the sideboards were not equipped with troop seats. The right side of the bed of the M36A2 swings down (drop-side) to allow forklift loading of cargo.

Photographed at Aberdeen Proving Ground, this M36A2 shows off the long lines of the 'extra long wheelbase' trucks, as well as the drop-side body configuration. The right-side panels hinge down in two sections. The sideboard extensions must be removed before lowering the side, and they are shown lying on the pavement beside the truck. (*Fred Crismon collection*)

This extra-long wheelbase cargo truck was used to distribute weapons and ammunition around Can Tho Airfield on 19 May 1970. The troops from the 235th Aviation Company, 307th Combat Aviation Battalion, 164th Combat Aviation Group. (*National Archives*)

The 190-inch wheelbase chassis was also used as the basis for the M292 family of expansible vans, such as this one. The structure over the cab roof contains a 240-volt, 3-phase air conditioner in the center, flanked by a fuel-burning heater on either side, which are connected to the exhaust stacks on the front of the box. A cable reel, wrapped in canvas, beneath the right-side of the body, contains a heavy electrical cable that is used to connect the van to a large trailer-mounted electrical generator, which the truck towed. (*Fred Crismon collection*)

When expanded, the large volume of space contained within an expansible van was utilized for logistics support, mapping, command and control, or other administrative functions. Typically, the work areas were fixed in the center of the body, with the volume gained by the expansion used for walkway, desk chairs, etc. (*Fred Crismon collection*)

The M109 series of trucks, such as this M109A2, as well as the similar M185 series vans, were considerably smaller than the M292 series, and were mounted on the 154-inch wheelbase M435 chassis. These bodies did not expand, nor did they come factory equipped with heat and air conditioning. The primary use of these vehicles was for maintenance workshops, such as small-arms repair. (*Fred Crismon collection*)

This M109, looking somewhat the worse for wear, is being towed by an M543-series wrecker. The van truck is being evaluated for retrograde and salvage on 8 November 1971. (*National Archives*)

The V17A/MTQ was a telephone-line maintenance truck built on the M44 chassis, featuring six 11.00-20 tires. Compartments both on the outside and inside of the body held tools and supply for telephone-line maintenance, while the structure on top of the body was a rotating maintenance platform with collapsible hand rails. The platform could be swung to the side of the truck, allowing direct access to telephone lines and poles. (*National Archives*)

Having arrived at the job site near Qui Nhon, Sgt. Joseph Boyd and Sp/4 Harold Martin gather the equipment that they need to work with. They are with the cable splicing section of HHC, 41st Signal Battalion, 12 Signal Group, 1st Signal Brigade. The large object on the inside-right body side of the truck is a collapsible cable reel, and secured to the floor at the left of the entrance to the bed is a pole jack, used to remove telephone poles. (*National Archives*)

While similar in appearance to the expansible van, this is a very different vehicle indeed. Popularly known as the ERDLator, this is a 1,500-gallon per hour water purification system. Mounted on the 154-inch wheelbase M435 chassis, this was a mobile water treatment plant, capable of converting ground water into potable water. A 3,000-gallon per hour model was also produced, using the the190-inch wheelbase M436 chassis. (*Fred Crismon collection*)

One side of the ERDLator opened to provide a working platform from which to operate the unit contained therein. These vehicles were equipped with heaters for the equipment area, and towed a trailer carrying a generator and other needed equipment. The name was derived from the Engineering Research and Development Laboratory, which developed the system. (*Fred Crismon collection*)

A 1,500-GPH ERDLator is set up near a pond adjacent to the motor pool area of the 2nd Battalion, 4th Artillery, 9th Infantry Division, at Tan An on 26 October 1967. (*National Archives*)

Since WWI, the US military has been concerned with chemical agents. On the battlefield certain chemical agents will linger on surfaces that they come in contact with, to the ill effect of troops subsequently touching or using the contaminated equipment. To counter this, various means of decontamination have been developed through the years, including this vehicle, designated the Decontaminating Apparatus, Power-Driven, Truck Mounted, M3A3 with Heater Unit. (*Chemical Corps History Office*)

Somewhat ironically, in Vietnam the Decontamination trucks were used to mix defoliants. Here, on 7 September 1967, one such truck is pumping defoliant aboard a UH-1D Huey which will then spray the chemicals on the jungle around the base camp of the 11th Armored Cavalry Regiment. (*National Archives*)

The 154-inch wheelbase chassis was used as the basis for several varieties of tactical firefighting trucks. The first of these, the Class 530A, had a front bumper-mounted pump, but the 530A was soon replaced by this, the Class 530B. The 530B featured a mid-ship mounted pump, driven by a full torque PTO which was attached to the truck's transfer case. The earliest 530Bs, like this example built by Fire Master, used the M44 chassis with six 11.00-20 tires. (*US Army Engineer School History Office*)

Known as tactical fire trucks, each Class 530B could be outfitted with one of three sets of tools and equipment, one for structural fires, one for aircraft fires, or one for brush fires, depending on the area the vehicle was to service and the anticipated predominate use. This 530B is involved trying to extinguish a fire resulting from the crash of a C-130 at An Khe on 12 March 1967. (*National Archives*)

Depending upon the 'security' of an area, the Class 530B, when in Army service, could be painted either Olive Drab, like the prior vehicle, or red, as is this truck photographed 20 March 1970, also at An Khe. (*National Archives*)

Later Class 530B trucks were built on Multifuel-powered M435 chassis, like this truck being evaluated at Fort Knox. (*Patton Museum*)

Vietnamese firefighters stow a three-section extension ladder in the rack atop a dual-wheel equipped 530B at Cam Rahn Bay on 14 January 1970. (*National Archives*)

The M54 family of 5-ton trucks, the G-744 series

The development path of the five-ton 6 × 6 of the Vietnam era, typified by the M54A1 cargo truck, paralleled that of the smaller, 2½-ton 6 × 6. The origins of the Cold War 5-ton 6 × 6 can be traced to the Cook Board Report of June 1945. The recommendations of that report were confirmed some five months later, in November 1945, by the Stilwell Board Report, a document that is more formally known as the Report of the War Department Equipment Board, a body that was under the chairmanship of General Joseph 'Vinegar Joe' Stilwell. Stilwell's board seconded the Cook Report's call to replace the wartime 4-ton 6 × 6 trucks – typified by the Diamond T 969 – with a 5-ton truck that featured power steering. Both of these boards expected the new 5-ton trucks to have a service life of five years. In 1950 the Army Equipment Board expressed the expectation that a new design for a cross-country carrier based on the T51 would replace the earlier conception of a 5-ton truck.

The document titled MCV 204, 'Military Characteristics of Vehicles, Truck, 5-ton, 6 × 6' spelled out the characteristics of the 'interim' design that would be designated G-744 in the military's Standard Nomenclature list. Although a solicitation for bids for these trucks, which were to be constructed in compliance with Joint Army-Navy Specification JAN T-72, was evidently issued, researchers in recent times have been unable to locate that document.

Shortly before the outbreak of the Korean War, the procurement of a new series of 5-ton trucks was the subject of meetings on 5 and 7 June 1950 of a board of officers that included Colonel Joseph Colby, Lieutenant Colonel George White, and Lieutenant Colonel John Cone. Board president Colonel David Crawford was not in attendance. Taking part were advisors to the board R.F. Brown and M.C. Morrison from the Detroit Arsenal, and C.R. Tobey from the Detroit Ordnance District.

Because the need for the trucks was so pressing, it was necessary to issue a contract for the vehicles, putting them into production before tests could be conducted on pilot models. Under consideration were trucks that would later achieve standardization as the M41 cargo truck and the M51 dump truck, however the cargo truck clearly received the lion's share of attention.

Concern over cost meant that discussion was immediately limited to proposals from the White Motor Company, Mack Manufacturing Company, and International Harvester. Engineering features, factors related to industrial mobilization, and cost of procurement were major considerations in the discussions. The vehicle proposed by Mack Manufacturing was eliminated first, since it had the highest cost, the least desirable engineering characteristics, and could cite no industrial mobilization advantage that could offset those serious drawbacks. For its part, White Motor Company required an eighty-day lead-time for production expansion, while International Harvester only asked for thirty days in the event of war. In addition, International had available manufacturing facilities in Fort Wayne, Indiana, and also in Springfield, Illinois, and Memphis, Tennessee, while White had only one production facility – in Cleveland, Ohio. From the standpoint of industrial mobilization, opting for International clearly had tremendous advantages.

The powerplant in the International truck was to be the Continental Engines' 602-cubic inch R6602, an engine previously tooled for a monthly output of 3,000 units. White's engine was only tooled at 1,000 units per month. International's truck design was also 500 pounds lighter than that of White, had 17 per cent greater torque, 10 per cent greater horsepower, and was, in every area of specification, considerably superior.

Only when it came to price was the White proposal ahead. The quoted price for the White truck was $10,183,737 for 910 vehicles, including preproduction models, but International Harvester's price for the same number of its vehicles was $10,367,567.

Although the board recognized the $184,000 cost advantage of the White proposal, the superiority of the design features of the IH truck together with that company's more extensive organization persuaded the board unanimously to recommend, on 7 June 1950, that contract DA-20-018-ORD-9197 be awarded to International Harvester Company. That contract stipulated delivery of 932 trucks. Then, with the Korean War in high gear, a follow-on order for 10,617 more of the vehicles was issued on 4 December that year. On that same day, another contract for a further 3,581 identical vehicles was awarded to the Diamond T Motor Car Company in Chicago, Illinois. The military placed yet another order for 1,665 more trucks with Mack Trucks on 29 June 1951. International's Ft. Wayne plant began actual manufacture of the trucks in January 1951. Throughout the decade of the 1950s, International, Mack and Diamond T continued to get orders for these vehicles. In the end, 48,639 trucks incorporating the Continental R6602 gasoline engine rolled off the assembly lines. International Harvester turned out 28,089 of the vehicles, Diamond T made 13,591 and Mack constructed 6,959.

Like Reo's 2½-ton M35, the 5-ton trucks had automatic front axle engagement with an overrunning clutch. Unlike the 2½-ton truck, in which a mechanical linkage was used to shift the sprag unit from forward to reverse, the 5-ton vehicle relied on an air cylinder to make this shift – an arrangement which, it might be noted, is not the same as that used for pneumatic engagement of the front axle that appeared on later versions of the M35.

Testing of the new trucks began at Aberdeen Proving Ground in March 1951, but it took until March 1953 for the trucks to receive the Standard A classification. Although they were rushed rather precipitously into production, the 5-ton trucks proved fundamentally satisfactory, as is seen from the fact that the basic design remained in production by various makers into the 1980s – a considerably longer duration than the originally predicted life span of only five years.

Among the first major changes to the basic design of the 5-ton truck was the introduction of a new, more fuel efficient engine. The Continental R6602 was powerful but consumed a great deal of gasoline. Mileage on the trucks when hauling heavy loads averaged only two miles per gallon. Army tests of a commercial truck powered by a Mack ENDT-673 engine highlighted the attractive potential offered by a tactical truck with diesel power. Accordingly, early in 1959, the Ordnance Tank Automotive Command (OTAC) called for several ENDT-673 engines be installed in the M54 6×6 truck for evaluation. Mack ENDT-673 engines were fitted in seven M54s in February 1960, resulting in seven test trucks with the designation M54E3.

A turbo-supercharged six-cylinder valve-in-head water-cooled compression-ignition diesel-engine, the ENDT-673 generated 211 gross brake horsepower at 2,100 revolutions per minute. Simultaneously with the installation of the diesel powerplant, a five-speed 6453 transmission was installed in place of the Spicer 6352 five-speed manual transmission. Both transmissions were five-speed models, but the 6453 transmissions boasted gear ratios more appropriate for the Mack powerplant, a relatively slow-turning engine.

Meanwhile, Cummins Model C200-A turbo-supercharged compression-ignition engines were installed in seven other trucks. These powerplants developed 200 gross brake horsepower at 2,800 revolutions per minute. The trucks that were repowered with the Cummins engine received the designation M54E4. The Aberdeen Proving Ground in Maryland, the Yuma Test Station in Arizona, and Fort Greely in Alaska were the arenas where the M54E3 and M54E4 underwent testing.

The M54E3 and the M54E4 both fulfilled all the standard specifications for 5-ton truck performance, but the general conclusion was drawn that the M54E3 had a slight edge over the Cummins competitor. Accordingly, in June 1962 the M54E3 received the Standard A classification and the designation M54A1.

M52 tractors and M54 cargo trucks were re-engined with the Mack ENDT-673 diesel powerplants under a program that began immediately after the engine reclassification and lasted until 1963. Mack Trucks and the Diamond T Motor Truck Company jointly carried out this conversion program. Diamond T installed the diesel engines in 5,356 existing cargo and tractor trucks. The vehicle model identifications for these trucks when equipped with the Diesel engine were M54A1 and M52A1 respectively.

This modification to incorporate diesel engines was, however, short-lived. After just one year, the decision was made to switch tactical fleet vehicles to Multifuel engines wherever possible. The LDS-465-1A was the Multifuel engine chosen for the 5-ton trucks. A turbo-supercharged version of the LD-465 that had been installed in 2½-ton trucks, the LDS-465-1A, featured added rings, better oiling and a different type of fuel-injection nozzle. The LDS-465's turbosupercharger, together with the different injector nozzles and fuel-injection pump settings, gave a boost that increased horsepower. This modification was more formidable than that achieved by the small turbo used on later 2½-ton trucks equipped with LDT engines. On those 2½-ton vehicles, the turbo simply cleaned up the exhaust. Otherwise there was nearly complete interchangeability of parts between the LD-465 and LDS-465, a fact that simplified the supply chain. Equipped with their new Multifuel engines, the cargo and tractor trucks' model suffixes were changed to A2.

The contract to manufacture the Multifuel version of the G-744 5-ton trucks was awarded to Studebaker in 1963. In the beginning, that contract covered provision of 4,159 trucks. Contract extensions later raised that number to 9,343 vehicles. Before manufacture of the trucks actually began, however, Kaiser Jeep purchased Studebaker's Chippewa Avenue truck plant, and with it the G-744 contract, in February 1964. In the following month, the contract transfer received US Army approval.

Contracts were awarded for a total of 44,490 Multifuel-powered 5-ton 6×6 trucks in all body types from June 1964 through March 1968, with all the vehicles manufactured in the South Bend plant. Kaiser-Jeep became the Jeep Corporation on 26 March 1970 and the South Bend plant became a part of the General Products Division. The General Products Division spun off to form AM General just over a year later: on 31 March 1971, but by then, the M54A2 was no longer being made. US personnel in Vietnam preferred the Mack powerplant over the Multifuel, regarding it as more powerful and reliable.

G-744 GENERAL DATA

MODEL	179' wheelbase cargo trucks	Dump truck	Tractor truck	Wrecker truck	Tractor-wrecker
WEIGHT NET^	19945	22663	18996	33325	32830
WEIGHT GROSS^	39945	42663	43996	45325	48830
MAX TOWED LOAD	15000	15000	30000	20000	20000
LENGTH*^	298.75	266.125	257.5	348	352
WIDTH*	97	97.25	97	97	97.5
HEIGHT*	116	110.625	103.125	127.125	132
WHEELBASE*	179	167	167	179	215
TIRE SIZE	11.00 – 20	11.00 – 20	11.00 – 20	11.00 – 20	12.00 – 20
MAX SPEED	52 mph	52 mph	52 mph	52 mph	52 mph
FUEL CAPY	78 gallons	110 gallons	110 gallons	78 gallons	78 gallons
RANGE LOADED	280 miles	440 miles	440 miles	200 miles	200 miles
ELECTRICAL	24 Neg	24 Neg	24 Neg	24 Neg	24 Neg
TRANSFER SPEEDS	2	2	2	2	2
TRANSMISSION SPEEDS	5 F	5 F	5 F	5 F	5 F
TURNING RADIUS FEET	20′ 7″	19′ 4½″	19′ 4½″	20′ 9½″	23′ 4″

All data given above are for gas powered trucks, for other powerplants please adjust as shown below. Data given for trucks less winch, except wreckers and tractor-wreckers, which all had front winches.

* Overall dimensions listed in inches.

^ Add 460 lbs to weight on vehicles powered by the ENDT-673 engine. Subtract 50 lbs from the gas powered vehicle weight for Multifuel engine powered trucks.

ENGINE DATA

ENGINE MAKE/MODEL	Continental R6602	Mack ENDT-673	LDS-465-1A
NUMBER OF CYLINDERS	6	6	6
CUBIC INCH DISPLACEMENT	602	672	478
HORSEPOWER	224	211	175
TORQUE	504 @ 1400	610 @ 1500	425 @ 2000

The US military's first type of 5-ton 6x6 was the International Harvester M41. The M41 was fitted with six 14.00-20 tires, consistent with the Army's doctrine of the time, which called for large single tires, rather than smaller duals, for improved off-road performance. In order to accommodate the large tires, the cargo bed had wheel wells in the floor. The five-ton 6x6 trucks of this type were given the Standard Nomenclature List (SNL) number of G-744. (*Patton Museum*)

Introduced shortly after the M41, the M54 was better suited for cargo, in that it lacked the wheel wells protruding in the bed. This was because the truck used smaller 11.00-20 tires, with dual rear wheels. (*Patton Museum*)

Due to increased fuel economy and torque, in 1959 the Army began serious consideration of Diesel power plants for the five-ton 6×6 truck family. This is one of twenty-two test vehicles equipped with the Mack ENDT-673 Diesel engine. The trial vehicles were designated M54E3, but once standardized for production the ENDT-673 powered vehicles were designated M54A1. (*Patton Museum*)

Only a year after the ENDT-673-powered M54A1 was standardized, that powerplant too was replaced as the Army moved to a multi-fuel powered tactical vehicle fleet. The cargo variant of the repowered 5-ton 6x6 was the M54A2, shown here, powered by a LDS-465 Multifuel engine. The trucks featured an air cleaner mounted on the right front fender, and a vertical exhaust pipe rising through the rear of the same fender. (*US Army Transportation Museum*)

A pallet of 8-inch howitzer ammunition is lifted from the bed of a 5-ton 6x6 somewhere in Vietnam during August 1969. The truck is towing an M332 ammunition trailer as well. (*National Archives*)

One of the workhorses of Engineer units was the M51 dump truck, a five-ton 6x6 of the G-744 series, powered by the R6602 six-cylinder Continental engine. At 167 inches, the wheelbase of the dump truck (and tractor truck) variants of the G-744 family were one foot shorter than the wheelbase of the cargo variants. (*International Harvester*)

Later models of the 5-ton dump truck were powered by the LDS-465 Multifuel engine, and were designated M51A2. This is the pilot for these trucks, the M51E5. (*Patton Museum*)

This convoy of 5-ton dump trucks loaded with crushed rock head for Dragon Mountain, near Pleiku, in April 1970. (*National Archives*)

Concrete pours from an M51A2 as part of a construction project in Vietnam as both GIs and Vietnamese level the surface. (*Carl T. Heller*)

The M328 bridge truck, built on the M139 chassis, was among the most imposing of the G-744 series vehicles, and also one of the few that were not built in Diesel or Multifuel-powered configurations. The trucks were intended specifically to transport and emplace components of portable floating bridge sections. (*International Harvester*)

The large roller at the end of the floor of the cargo bed was intended to aid in the loading and unloading of the bridge components. This truck has been unloaded and a section of culvert placed in the front of the cargo bed, forming a makeshift gun emplacement. Members of the 4th Infantry Detachment (War Dog Provisional) are using the oversize truck as a transport into the combat area from Camp Enari in February 1969. (*National Archives*)

Not surprisingly, with such a vast fleet of vehicles, the military has a need for tow and recovery vehicles. For the US Army in Vietnam, this was the mainstay of this type of equipment – the M543 5-ton 6x6. The Austin-Western hydraulic crane, which could rotate through about 270 degrees, and could be extended hydraulically from 10 to 18 feet, was used for lifting loads up to 20,000 pounds. In addition, each truck was equipped with a 45,000-pound capacity rear recovery winch, as well as a 20,000-pound capacity front mounted self-recovery winch. (*Mike Haines collection*)

An M543A2 has an 11th Cav M51A2 dump truck 'on the hook' somewhere in Vietnam. On the side of the boom, also known as the shipper, is mounted a large tank that is the hydraulic reservoir for the crane, which could raise, lower, extend and rotate. (*Chris Harlow*)

The Marines did not embrace hydraulic wreckers as quickly as did the Army, utilizing instead the M40 wrecker equipped with a twin boom Holmes 850 bed. Each boom was rated with a lifting capacity of 20,000 pounds and a line pull of 35,000 pounds. (*USMC*)

A USMC M40 returns to base with the remains of an M35A2 apparently destroyed in an ambush. (*James Lyles collection*)

The M246 was a combination crane and truck tractor, intended to be used in retrieving damaged aircraft. The vehicle could tow a long low bed trailer, and the crane would lift and place the errant aircraft on the towed trailer. (*TACOM LCMC History Office*)

On 12 April 1965 this M246 drove off a landing craft onto a beach in Vietnam. The 5-ton, 6×6 tractor-wrecker truck had a 215-inch wheelbase and was equipped with 12.00-20 tires and dual rear wheels. The crane boom could be extended from 11½ to 26 feet, could be used to lift loads up to 20,000 pounds. (*National Archives*)

The truck-tractor version of the G744 family was the M52. Like the other G744 trucks, the M52 was initially powered by the gasoline-burning Continental R6602 six-cylinder engine. The M52 had a 167-inch wheelbase, and was fitted with 11.00-20 tires. A fifth wheel assembly, approach plates, and deck plate, suitable for hauling trailers, were mounted on the rear of the chassis. Tractor-to-trailer brake hoses and connections were mounted behind the cab. (*Mack Museum*)

Like the cargo trucks, the tractor trucks went through an evolution of powerplants, with first the Mack ENDT-673 engine and later the LDS-465 Multifuel engine being used in place of the R6602. Here, one of these later trucks pulls equipment off a landing craft at Vung Ro Bay in September 1966. (*National Archives*)

The five-ton tractors saw extensive use in line haul operations throughout Vietnam. Here, trailers are being loaded with 8-inch howitzer ammunition at Qui Nhon, on 3 September 1966. With no fender-mounted air cleaner visible, this appears to be a straight gasoline-fueled M52. (*National Archives*)

The Corps of Engineers fielded mobile machine shops mounted on the 5-ton 6 x 6 chassis. Featuring a welder/generator driven by the truck engine, these shops were equipped with a lathe, grinder, drill presses and an array of hand tools. With the equipment aboard, the skilled men issued these vehicles were equipped to perform major repairs in the field. (*National Archives*)

The M123 family of 10-ton trucks, the G-792 series

Many of the chassis components of the WWII-era NO series 7½-ton prime movers' chassis components were used in the trucks of the G-792 series. The massive Le Roi TH-844 V-8 gasoline engine chosen for the G-792s initially powered both the tractor and the prime mover. Non-synchronized combination transmission and transfer cases were used in the trucks. These components, as well as the vehicles' axles, were designed and produced by Mack.

Manufacture of the M123 10-ton tractor was launched by Mack in 1955. Mack produced multiple variants of the trucks. Fifth wheels made to accept 3.5-inch kingpins are a feature of all the trucks in the series, but the fifth-wheel mountings vary, as does the arrangement of the rear 45,000-pound capacity winch. None of the tractors featured front-mounted winches – a difference from the M125 prime mover.

Dual rear winches and a normally mounted fifth wheel were features of the basic M123. Single winches and low-mounted fifth wheels were features of the M123C. Dual winches and a low-mounted fifth wheel were features of the M123D. The big Le Roi gasoline engine powered all of these trucks. Although at the time the M123 was being designed the Army was hoping to move on to a multifuel engine series, the Le Roi was chosen as the best alternative. The massive powerplant with its 844-cubic inch displacement was thirsty, however. Mileage failed to attain even two miles per gallon.

A more efficient alternative engine was soon being sought and eventually the Cummins V8-300 diesel was adopted. A uniquely military engine, the V8-300 outwardly seemed closely to resemble the VT-903 civilian powerplant, but was in fact almost completely different. The diesel had a slightly smaller displacement – 785 cubic inches – than the earlier gasoline engine, and offered slightly improved fuel economy, while delivering essentially the same horsepower.

The need for more tank transports escalated in keeping with the expansion of the war in Indochina. Accordingly, in June 1965, a contract was awarded to Consolidated Diesel Electric Company (CONDEC) of Old Greenwich, Connecticut. Consolidated Diesel was to produce under the contract 1,848 diesel-powered versions of the M123A1C truck. This vehicle incorporated the V8-300 Cummins powerplant and employed the same Mack axles and combination transmission and transfer case. In June 1967, a contract for 1,340 more of the vehicles was awarded to CONDEC.

Mack returned to the scene in June 1968 when it was awarded a contract to make 420 M123A1C trucks. A contract to manufacture 210 M123E2 vehicles was awarded simultaneously. The vehicles covered under the document were the remanufactures of 210 of the gasoline-engine trucks as diesel-powered vehicles with dual rear winches. During 1969 the conversions were made.

The speed range of the Cummins engine differed from that of the Le Roi, and downshifting was noticeably more difficult. As a result, Williams Exhaust Brakes were retrofitted on many of these tractors; 10-ton tractors initially hauled the M15A2 50-ton trailer, but later these trucks also pulled M172A2, M162, M793 and M747 semi-trailers.

G-792 GENERAL DATA

MODEL	M123A1C
WEIGHT NET	29100
LENGTH*	280
WIDTH*	114
HEIGHT*	108
TIRE SIZE	14.00-24
MAX SPEED	45 mph
FUEL CAPY	166 gallons
RANGE	350 miles
ELECTRICAL	24 V NEG
TRANSMISSION SPEEDS	5 FWD, 1 REV
TRANSFER SPEEDS	2

* Overall dimensions listed in inches.

ENGINE DATA

ENGINE MAKE/MODEL	Cummins V9-300
NUMBER OF CYLINDERS	8
CUBIC INCH DISPLACEMENT	785
HORSEPOWER	300 @ 3000 rpm
TORQUE	580 @ 2100 rpm

In the early 1950s, Mack developed two new 10-ton 6×6 vehicles in the G-792 series: the M123, a truck-tractor, and the M125, a cargo truck. These vehicles were the heaviest tactical vehicles fielded by the United States Army in the early postwar years. The M123 featured the Reo-designed cab that also was used on the G-742 2 1/2-ton trucks and the G-744 5-ton trucks. Shown here is the prototype XM123. (*Mack Museum*)

An improved version of the M123 truck-tractor, the M123A1C, was produced starting in the mid-1960s. These were powered by the Cummins V8-300 diesel engine. A characteristic differentiating the M123A1C from the M123 was the elbow-shaped air intake on the right side of the hood for the new, single air cleaner in the engine compartment. The vehicle shown here was from the 1968 production year. (*Mack Museum*)

In 1968, Mack was contracted to convert 210 gasoline-engine 10-ton 6×6 truck-tractors to diesel-powered. These vehicles, designated the M123E2, received Cummins V8-300 engines, and they featured dual winches to the rear of the cab. The fifth wheel seen here is the low-mount version, with the trunnion brackets mounted directly to the top of the chassis frame. (*TACOM LCMC History Office*)

An M123A1C 10-ton truck-tractor, right, is parked next to a M51A2 5-ton 6×6 dump truck to show the difference in size and appearance. Both types of vehicles shared the same cab and front clip, but the M123A1C rode higher, largely due to its beefier suspension and bigger tires. The M123A1 was assigned to Company D, 31st Engineer Battalion, 34th Engineer Group (Construction), 20th Engineer Brigade, which served in Vietnam in the late 1960s. (*Chris Harlow*)

This Diesel-powered 10-ton 6×6 truck tractor of Company D, 557th Engineer Battalion, 18th Engineer Brigade, 35th Engineer Group, photographed at the battalion's motor pool, has amber-colored service-headlight lenses. Two swivel sheaves are visible above the cab top, suggesting this vehicle may have been an M123E2. (*Harry C. Dunlap via Military Vehicles Magazine*)

M123A1C 10-ton tractors and dozers fill the motor park of the 984th Land Clearing Company, 62nd Engineer Battalion, 79th Engineer Group, at Long Binh, Republic of Vietnam, on 21 April 1970. In the center background a Rome plow with a large yellow number 5 on the side of it is being loaded on a semi-trailer coupled to a 10-ton 6×6 truck-tractor. 'Watch your step' is stenciled on the bottom of the driver's door of the tractor in the foreground. (*National Archives*)

GOER

In the years immediately following WWII the United States Military branches developed a wide array of tactical vehicles. This unprecedented growth began even before the war's end with designs for new generations of vehicles. Vehicles were sought with greatly increased load carrying capacity and enhanced ability in extreme off-road conditions. The United States Armored Board felt that construction equipment might serve as a basis for tactical vehicles, and began evaluating large-wheeled earth-moving equipment in 1956.

Tests of a number of commercial vehicles with articulated steering began in 1957. Several development contracts for 4×4 all-terrain vehicles of several weight classes were awarded based on the results. Clark Equipment provided a prototype in the 5-ton weight class. LeTourneau-Westinghouse supplied three variants of a 15-ton class vehicle: the XM437 cargo vehicle, XM438 tanker, and XM554 wrecker. None of these vehicles saw series production.

The Caterpillar Tractor Company provided an 8-ton class prototype. With a lengthy history of military designs dating back to WWI's Holt Tractor, and substantial experience with heavy articulated vehicles, Caterpillar's vehicle performed well. A $5 million contract was awarded Caterpillar in 1960 to design and build eight vehicles, which they delivered during 1961 and 1962. The vehicles were designated GOER – for Go-Ability with Overall Reliability. Along with these cargo trucks, contracts were added in 1962 for two 10-ton wreckers and two 2,500-gallon tanker trucks.

Caterpillar was awarded contracts in May of 1963 for thirteen XM520 cargo vehicles, eight XM559 tankers and two XM553 wreckers. The vehicles in this contract were destined for service tests. Units in Germany put these vehicles through extensive trials during 1964. At the end of this trial period, during which the vehicles accumulated 66,504 miles, they were stored in an Army Depot in Germany. A year later they were reconditioned and sent to Vietnam for further testing, the first two vehicles arriving at Cam Ranh Bay in August 1966. Shortly after the arrival in Vietnam the GOERs were used to support the 4th Infantry Division during monsoon season, easily negotiating 3 to 4 foot deep mud.

Finally, in May 1971, Caterpillar Tractor Co. was awarded a production contract due to the vehicles' successful performance. The contract was for 812 M520 cargo vehicles, 117 M553 wreckers and 371 M559 tankers. Production began in 1971, and final deliveries were made in June 1976.

The GOER consisted of a front and a rear section connected with an articulated joint in the center, similar to commercial earth moving equipment. The joint gave a steering angle up to 60 degrees and permitted lateral oscillation of up to 20 degrees.

The engine was housed in the forward section behind the crew area. The driver was on the left side of the cab, with the vehicle commander to the right. The vehicle was equipped with a moveable windshield, as well as a removable canvas top with side curtains.

Engine power was transmitted through a six-speed gear box. A short drive shaft connected the transmission to the front differential, which transmitted power to planetary units within each of the front hubs.

The front differential drove the rear through a connecting clutch, drive shafts and universal joints. Planetary gears were also used for the final drives within the rear hubs. The rear wheels are driven automatically in the two lower gears. A system automatically disengaged the rear wheels as the transmission shifted up to third gear, although this could be manually over ridden by the operator.

The GOERs were fully amphibious in spite of their massive size. The vehicle was propelled in the water by its wheels. Special kits were developed for the vehicles, including a wheel chain kit, trailer brake kit, arctic kit, machine gun kit and infra-red driving kit.

The rear section of the M520 was made up largely of the cargo bed. The bed was of a corrugated construction, with doors at the side and rear to allow rapid loading and unloading of cargo. To preserve the amphibious ability of the vehicle the cargo doors were equipped with watertight seals. The cargo area was capable of carrying twenty-five 55-gallon drums, or six standard military pallets. One CONEX container could also be carried along with two military pallets.

The recessed area at the front panel of the cab was fitted with a standard military-type Gar Wood 10,000 pound winch. The M877 was the designation of the GOER equipped with a folding crane for the handling of cargo.

M553 Wrecker

The M553 wrecker was similar in layout to the M520 cargo model. The rear cargo area was replaced by various recovery equipment including a hydraulically operated crane.

The crane had a maximum lifting capacity of between 10,000 and 20,000 pounds depending on the extension of the boom. The boom was 6 feet in length and could be extended out to 16 feet. Hydraulic pressure was supplied by a hydraulic pump coupled to the engine crankshaft. The vehicle was stabilized by outriggers during recovery operations.

The cab of the M553 was also equipped with a 10,000 pound capacity self-recovery Gar Wood winch in the same position as the M520 cargo model.

M559 2,500-gallon fuel tanker

The M559 tanker variant featured a 2,500-gallon stainless steel tank. It was fitted with a large pump, a military aircraft fuel filler, four pressure discharge outlets, three discharge hoses and a large bulk outlet. All three hoses could be discharged simultaneously. For handling bulk fuel the tanker was equipped with a gravity discharge outlet.

Though the use of the GOER during the Vietnam War was considered successful, it was not long for service with the military. The vehicles were awkward to use on hard surfaced roads, as well as being oversized. The GOER was replaced by the HEMTT, which combined off-road heavy transport mobility with adequate road performance. A demilitarization order similar to that of the M151 was required of surplus GOERs. Vehicles that exist in private collections have been reassembled and critical driveline and steering components replaced.

G-561 GENERAL DATA

MODEL	M520	M553	M559
WEIGHT NET GROSS	25430 41400	37870 45780	28100 46550
MAX TOWED LOAD	20000	20000	20000
LENGTH*	380	401.75	375.75
WIDTH*	108	108	108
HEIGHT*	133.5	139.5	133.5
TIRE SIZE	18.00 x 33	18.00 X 33	18.00 x 33
MAX SPEED LAND	30 mph	30 mph	30 mph
MAX SPEED WATER	2.8 mph	2.6 mph	2.6 mph
FUEL CAPY	106 gallons	106 gallons	106 gallons
RANGE	300 miles	300 miles	300 miles
ELECTRICAL	24 volt	24 volt	24 volt
TRANSMISSION SPEEDS	6	6	6
TURNING RADIUS FEET	52.7	52.7	52.7

* Overall dimensions listed in inches.

ENGINE DATA

ENGINE MAKE/MODEL	Caterpillar D33T
NUMBER OF CYLINDERS	6
CUBIC INCH DISPLACEMENT	638
HORSEPOWER	213 @ 2200 rpm
TORQUE	578 @ 1550 rpm

The M520 GOER was driven by a Caterpillar D333 inline six-cylinder diesel engine coupled to a six-speed transmission with torque converter and planetary drive. The vehicle had a rated cross-country load capacity of 8 tons. The tires used on these vehicles, huge 18.00 x 33 ten-ply off-road tires, also doubled as the vehicles' suspension system. (*TACOM LCMC History Office*)

The prototype vehicles such as this XM520E1 can be distinguished from production vehicles by the prototype's smooth outer cab panels and the door-like arrangement protecting the front winch. The heart of the GOER's off-road ability was the flexible coupling between the power unit and trailer. This coupling permitted 20 degree movement and roll, and 60 degrees of articulation, which resulted in the GOER having a 53-foot turning radius. (*Ordnance Museum*)

The side-loading doors of the GOER sealed completely when closed, permitting the huge vehicle to swim in still water. Water propulsion was provided by the churning wheels, which could move the vehicle at 2 to 8 mph on calm surfaces. (*TACOM LCMC History Office*)

Cargo variants of the GOER were 31 feet, 8-inches long, and were just over 8 feet tall. The 105 gallons of fuel, divided into two tanks, gave it a range of approximately 300 miles. Top speed was listed as 31 mph, though the lack of suspension and the large earthmover tires tended to cause control problems, leading most operators to hold speeds in the 20s. This M520 was photographed in Qui Nhon, Vietnam, on 10 September 1968, while in service with the 444th Transportation Company, 27th Transportation Battalion, 8th Group. (*National Archives*)

During driver training and vehicle testing at Pleiku in July 1967, this M520 easily negotiates a deep, water-filled mud pit that would have immobilized most other type vehicles. (*National Archives*)

When fitted with a materials handling crane, the M520 was designated M877. Despite the three large cargo doors (one each at rear and each side) found on cargo GOERs, this crane was invaluable to expedite unloading in combat areas, where time is critical. (*National Archives*)

The Marinette Marine plant also produced 371 of the M559 fuel tanker variant. This M559 is leaving the factory aboard a rail car; the vehicles would be oversize for highway transport. Fully loaded, these tankers tipped the scales at 46,550 pounds. Like all the other GOERs, the M559 was 108 inches wide. (*TACOM LCMC History Office*)

This M559 was photographed in Qui Nhon, Vietnam, on 10 September 1968, while in service with the 444th Transportation Company, 27th Transportation Battalion, 8th Group. The fuel tankers were especially useful as they could bring fuel to essentially any unit or vehicle anywhere. (*National Archives*)

A M559 GOER tanker of the GOER Transportation Company, 88th Services and Supply Command Support, 1st Logistical Command, operates with 5-ton 6x6s near Pleiku in August 1967. (*National Archives*)

The 117 production models of the M553 had the corrugated cab panels characteristic of the 1971–76 procurement. By using the GI as a gauge, the size of these unorthodox vehicles can be appreciated. A full array of recovery and repair equipment was carried on the M553, including two spare tires. Other GOER vehicles were not equipped with spare tires as their crews did not have the means of changing them. Though removed in this photo, all M553 vehicles were equipped with a front-mounted self-recovery winch. (*TACOM LCMC History Office*)

Though the M553 retained the large side cargo doors of the M520, the same cannot be said for the rear door. In its place was a much smaller door, through which could be played the cable of the rear drag winch. Intended for recovering mired sister vehicles, the hydraulically powered winch, built by Pacific Car and Foundry, had a 45,000 pound capacity. It was controlled electrically through a tether. (*TACOM LCMC History Office*)

A M553 GOER wrecker negotiates the mud pit in the GOER training area at Pleiku on 16 July 1967. The cab portions of the M520 and the M877 were identical, whereas the cab of the M553 – as well as that of the M559 – differed. The cab sections of the later two vehicles included the necessary power takeoffs and controls for operating the specialized equipment housed in their trailers. Warning beacons are mounted above the windshield on the tractor unit. (*National Archives*)

The LARC-V

Although the DUKW of WWII was generally considered to have been a success, the Army sought a vehicle with greater cargo capacity. The Drake was a postwar attempt at an enlarged DUKW. Eventually a clean slate design was developed for a much larger amphibious cargo vehicle with a 5-ton capacity, the LARC-V, the acronym standing for 'Lighter, Amphibious Resupply, Cargo, 5-ton'.

Often considered as a modern replacement for the WWII-era DUKW, the LARC-V is in reality a much larger vehicle (although smaller than its siblings – the LARC-XV and the LARC-LX, or BARC). The Army Research Command began work on developing the vehicle in 1956, and a prototype was ready in July 1959. Production began in 1963 after a period of testing and modification.

The LARC-V is 35-feet long, 10-foot wide, and weighs in at 19,000 lbs. and its body is constructed completely of aluminum. It was powered by a V8-300 Cummins diesel engine located at the rear of the hull and was equipped with an automatic transmission. The vehicles much more resemble a boat with wheels than a cargo truck.

The Adams Division of LeTourneau-Westinghouse was the initial manufacturer of hull numbers 9 through 241. Consolidated Diesel Electric assembled the vehicles from hull number 242 and continuing through hull number 968. There are minor detail differences between vehicles of the two manufacturers.

The crew cab was on the upper front of the vehicle with the steering controls in the center. The cab could be enclosed with either a hard or soft top. The steering was hydraulically assisted. Lengthy training was required to properly operate the vehicle, particularly during amphibious use. The engine was in the rear of the vehicle and transmitted power forward through a single speed transmission. A two-speed transfer case drove the four wheels through a series of right-angle drives and planetary hubs. The cargo area in the center deck was equipped with side curtains to protect cargo from the surf.

The vast majority of the LARC-Vs were assigned to Army units with only a few going to the Navy and Coast Guard. The LARC-V saw considerable service in the Vietnam War, equipping the 165th, 305th, 344th, 458th, and 461st Trans Companies. The Army's vehicles were disposed of after that war, with many being destroyed overseas rather than shipping them back to the US.

GENERAL DATA

MODEL	LARC-V
WEIGHT NET Gross	19000 30000
LENGTH*	420
WIDTH*	120
HEIGHT*	122
TIRE SIZES	18.00x25
MAX SPEED LAND WATER	30 9.5
FUEL CAPY	144
RANGE	250
ELECTRICAL	24 Negative
TRANSMISSION SPEEDS	1
TRANSFER SPEEDS	2
TURNING RADIUS FEET	41.25

* Overall dimensions listed in inches.
# inside/outside width at tires.

ENGINE DATA

ENGINE MAKE/MODEL	Cummins V8-300
NUMBER OF CYLINDERS	8
CUBIC INCH DISPLACEMENT	785
HORSEPOWER	300 @ 3000

The LARC-V, the V indicating a 5-ton capacity, was developed for rapid ship-to-shore movement of cargo and personnel, along with the ability to move inland from sea as necessary. This LARC-V is demonstrating its cargo capacity by transporting a Dodge M37. (*TACOM LCMC History Office*)

The 344th Transportation Company was the first unit to receive the LARC-V in Vietnam. On 5 June 1965, fifty of the vehicles including the one pictured arrived on the USNS *Comet*, and were then used to unload the ship. This example was built by Consolidated Diesel Electric (CONDEC), who produced the largest number of the vehicles. (*National Archives*)

This LARC-V, as was often the case in Vietnam, is loaded with a CONEX container, and the side curtains have been raised in preparation of entering the water. The LARC-V's cargo compartment could hold one Type II (295 cubic feet) or two Type I (135 cubic foot) CONEX boxes. This example was produced by the Adams Division of LeTourneau-Westinghouse. (*TACOM LCMC History Office*)

A CONDEC LARC-V itself is offloaded from the USNS *Comet* off the coast of Qui Nhon. The CONDEC-built vehicles can be distinguished by the 'railings' on the cargo decks – actually load centering devices to guide CONEX boxes. (*National Archives*)

An overhead view of a CONDEC vehicle receiving small cargo-containers of acid at Qui Nhon. The grille design varied slightly between the two manufacturers. Note the canvas cover in place over the two-seat operator's cabin. (*National Archives*)

LARC-Vs of the 344th begin to reach shore after a seven mile voyage. With a 10,000 pound cargo there was a 10-inch freeboard amidships. A top speed of 10 mph could be reached by the LARC-V in calm seas. (*National Archives*)

The LARC LX, or BARC

The Barge Amphibious Resupply Cargo (BARC) was developed in the early 1950s and remains one of the largest land vehicles fielded by any army. This was a period in the United States when all things got bigger: houses, automobiles, highways. Brigadier General Frank Schaffer Besson championed the development of several vehicles including the BARC, LARC-V and LARC-XV.

Besson was an advocate of modern containerization, streamlined ocean terminal practices, and of roll on/roll off methods of moving vehicles. The BARC fit these parameters, and given its huge size, it gained the nickname of 'Besson's Ark'.

The BARC had a cargo capacity of 60 tons, and could carry containers and wheeled and tracked vehicles, from ship to shore. The BARC could operate in breaking surf and could drive over low-strength soils.

Pacific Car and Foundry produced the initial prototypes of the BARC and began testing them at Fort Lawton, Washington in 1952. Four massive diesel engines were required to propel the vehicle which had an empty weight of 97½ tons, one powering each tire on land. Four Detroit Diesel 6-71 six-cylinder diesel engines were housed in the side walls of the vehicle. The two engines on each side of the machine were coupled to the propeller on the same side while in the water.

The production vehicles were manufactured by four fi rms, Treadwell Construction Company, Transval Electronic Corp, Western Gear Corp., and Peterson Builders.

The BARC was capable of attaining 20 mph on land, or 7½ mph in the calm water, despite its size and weight. The large ramp which made up the majority of the front of the vehicle allowed the rapid unloading of vehicles and general cargo.

The BARC was redesignated the LARC LX, or Lighter, Amphibious, Resupply, Cargo, 60 ton in 1960. In 1967, when BARCs were deployed to Vietnam, they proved Besson's plan and the quality of the vehicle's design. The BARCs began transporting cargo from ships off shore onto Wunder Beach, at times operating around the clock.

In the late 1970s, a faster means of ship-to-shore transport was sought by the US Army. The LACV-30 was the end product of these efforts. Many in the Army felt that the proven LARC-LX was a better choice than these new vehicles. Despite its comparatively low speed the LARC-LX was capable of moving tanks, which the LACV-30 could not do, plus it had double the cargo capacity. Eventually the LARC-LX lost out and on 15 October 2001, the last LARC-LX unit, the Army's 309th Transportation (LARC-LX) Company, 11th Transportation Battalion, was deactivated.

The US Army's BARC (Barge Amphibious Resupply Cargo) was designed with a cargo capacity of 60 tons. Its four tires had a diameter of 9½ feet. Each tire was powered by a 265-horsepower GMC 71-series two-stroke marine diesel engine on land. In the water two engines on each side were coupled to one propeller. The BARC could carry a fully equipped infantry company or a variety of other loads of up to 60 tons (and, reportedly, up to 100 tons on a limited basis). The vehicle had a length of 63 inches, a beam of 27 feet, and the cargo deck had an area of 527 square feet. The cabin near the bow identifies this as an early production BARC. The bow and the side of this craft are marked with the insignia of the US Army Transportation Corps, and the marking 'TRADS' stands for the Transportation Research and Development Station. (*US Army Transportation Museum*)

The first BARC is seen alongside a DUKW at the key presentation ceremony at the Boeing plant in Renton, Washington, on 8 September 1952. Two of the three port engine compartment covers are raised, giving easy access to the engines and related equipment. The large, wide tires provided very low ground pressure, enabling the BARC to negotiate unstable (or 'low-strength') surfaces impassable to other types of amphibious vehicles. The four wheels being steerable allowed the vehicle to travel at a 30-degree angle to its front-rear axis. (*US Army Transportation Museum*)

Three LARC-LX (Lighter Amphibious Resupply Cargo 60-ton), as the BARC was re-designated in 1960, dominate this scene in the inner harbor of Qui Nhon on 21 September 1966. The BARC was the only amphibious vehicle in US Army service during the Cold War era capable of landing through breaking surf. One report states that the BARC could land in a 15′ surf. (*US Army Transportation Museum*)

A LARC-LX coming ashore with supplies near Duc Pho, Quang Ngai Province, Republic of Vietnam, on 13 May 1967. The vehicle numbered '23' was part of Task Force Gallagher, transporting supplies from a US Navy Landing Ship, Tank (LST) unit to elements of the 1st Brigade, 101st Airborne Division and 3rd Brigade Task Force, 25th Infantry Division. The cabin on the left-rear of the vehicle identifies this as a late production BARC/LARC-LX. The frame-and-canvas enclosure over the rear deck, as seen on this example, was commonplace in Vietnam. (*National Archives*)

Finished unloading its cargo, this LARC-LX prepares to back into the surf for the return trip to an LST on 13 May 1967. Details of the wooden frame and planking of the rear-deck enclosure and the canvas top and sunshades are visible. Tires are used, tied to the gunwales, to protect the vehicle from the battering it would receive when approaching or moored to the supply ships. This later production BARC has different engine compartment covers, featuring a lower profile and spaces between the covers. (*National Archives photo*)

A LARC-LX is loaded with a 5-ton M52-series tractor and a 5,000-gallon tanker trailer of the 1st Logistical Command during the Task Force Gallagher resupply mission, 13 May 1967. The fuel trailer would then be filled by a tanker ship offshore before the LARC returned to the beach. The nonstandard enclosure of this LARC-LX does not cover the cabin as on other vehicles. (*National Archives photo*)

The Cadillac Gage Commando

Modern looking for a vehicle developed in 1962, and its descendants of the 4 × 4 Commando continue in service the world over, the Commando was developed as a private venture rather than as a result of an invitation for bids by the military.

Development of the vehicle was done by Cadillac Gage's Terra-Space division, with the initial prototype being completed in June 1962. Sales literature was aimed at not only national governments, but local governments and municipalities as well. These brochures promoted the vehicle for riot control, security and convoy escort roles – all of which it would ultimately fulfill.

The Commando prototype vehicle featured eleven protruding vision blocks identical to those on the M113 and small doors in the upper portion of each hull side. These doors proved too small for combat-laden troops to easily use. Much larger two-piece side doors, with the upper portion swinging up, were therefore added to further prototypes, with the lower portion swinging down and forming a step. At this time a large single-piece upward-opening door was added to the rear of the vehicle. It was replaced by a two-piece door similar to that on the sides once field experience showed that the large rear door was too difficult for Vietnamese soldiers to use.

Given the Cadillac Gage model number V-100, the Commando went through a number of changes during production, resulting in many variations, beyond the obvious model changes. The hulls of the first seventy-five vehicles had angular wheel-well cutouts. Field use soon demonstrated that the sharp corners of this design concentrated stress in the Cadaloy armor plate, leading to cracks emanating from these corners. With the production of the seventy-sixth vehicle a semi-circular wheel well cutout was introduced. At this time a large hatch was also added to the left side of the vehicle, permitting additional access to the engine compartment, which previously could only be serviced through a rooftop hatch.

Sequence production began at serial number 10000, and at number 10457 the air intake began to be shielded as a defense against Molotov cocktails. At serial number 10509 the flat plate hatches over the driver's and commander's heads gave way to raised hatches providing additional headroom. To strengthen the hull, one each of the vision blocks and firing ports was eliminated from each side at serial number 10596, due to combat experience gained in Vietnam.

The Ex-Cell-O Corporation owned Cadillac Gage by 1965, and the Terra-Space name was forgotten. The Cadillac Gage name now being affixed to the all Commando vehicles and literature. V-100 Commandos began to be purchased by outside nations, initially by Oman, Somalia and Sudan, then followed by orders from other Third World and Arabic nations. The most notable customer was the Republic of South Vietnam.

The US Advanced Research Projects Agency purchased the second and third pilot models and shipped them to South Vietnam in September 1963. The US Army Tank Automotive Command had purchased the first pilot for testing in the United States. The field trials proved that the Commando was indeed suitable for use in Vietnam, with some minor design changes. In addition to changes mentioned earlier, a recommendation was made for the replacement of the conventional non-directional cross-country tire with one of a self-cleaning tread design. Cadillac Gage responded with the Commando Special, their own tire design. These run-flat tires had a chevron tread pattern, with a wire-reinforced sidewall and a steel liner. While making the tires extraordinarily difficult to change, this design did allow the vehicle to be operated up to 50 miles on a flat. The vehicles were not furnished with spare tires nor jacks due to the fitment of the run-flat tires.

During vehicle development, turrets went through design changes, as did the hulls. Four different turret types were tried on the prototype vehicle. The T50 turret with twin machine guns fitted in the gunner's position was eventually fitted to all production vehicles. Installed on the XM706, this turret could be fitted with either two .30 caliber machine guns, or a .30 and a .50 caliber. A 7.62mm M73 machine gun replaced the .30 caliber on M706 models.

V-100 Commandos initially supplied to South Vietnam were designated XM706. The vehicle was re-designated XM706E1 with changes made at serial number 10596, and was later standardized in US service as the M706.

A turretless version of the Commando appeared in Cadillac Gage literature in 1967, and the United States Air Force procured this version, the XM706E2, for base security. In place of the turret was an armored parapet that could be closed by means of bifold doors. Five mounting-points for machine guns were provided on the parapet walls.

The first US combat use of the Commando was with vehicles on loan from the Army of the Republic of Vietnam. Their successful use prompted the US procurement of the vehicle. The 720th and 504th Military Police Battalions were among the first users, employing them in convoy escort and base security roles. Generally the vehicles were fielded with a two-man crew, a driver and a gunner.

The same engine that was being used in the M113 armored personnel carrier at the time was used in the production model Commando. The engine was a Chrysler gasoline V-8 with a 361 cubic inch displacement. The V-100 used axles based on those found in the G-742 series (M35-style) 2½-ton trucks with the addition of a no-slip differential. A five-speed New Process transmission was bolted to the back of the engine. To prevent the breaking of rear axles, an interlock prevented the use of low gear unless the single-speed transfer case was in the four-wheel drive position. Eighty gallons of fuel was carried in twin tanks. The Vehicles top speed was rated at 62 mph with an on-road range of up to 500 miles. At the front of the vehicle, a 10,000-pound rated Braden self-recovery winch was mounted internally.

All versions of the Commando were amphibious and could enter the water without special preparation. Propulsion was provided in the water by the turning wheels. Any leaks were dealt with by a bilge pump with a capacity of 50 gallons per minute.

After America's withdrawal from Vietnam the Commando saw limited use by US forces despite its success. A few went through a rebuild program for use as security vehicles in Europe. Others were surplused to large cities for use as riot control vehicles, or by police SWAT (Special Weapons and Tactics) teams.

GENERAL DATA

MODEL	XM706	M706	XM706E2
WEIGHT^	13800	13800	13300
LENGTH*	224	224	224
WIDTH*	89	89	89
HEIGHT*	96	96	96
CREW	UP TO 11	UP TO 11	UP TO 11
TIRE SIZES	14.00-20	14.00-20	14.00-20
MAX SPEED	60 mph	60 mph	60 mph
FUEL CAPY	80 gallons	80 gallons	80 gallons
RANGE	400 miles	400 miles	400 miles
ELECTRICAL	24 negative ground	24 negative ground	24 negative ground
TRANSMISSION SPEEDS	5F 1R	5F 1R	5F 1R
TRANSFER SPEEDS	1	1	1
TURNING RADIUS FEET	27	27	27
ARMAMENT	2x .30 cal. or 2x 7.62 mm MG73 or 1x .50 cal. & 1x .30 cal.	2x 7.62 mm M73	Pintle mounts for 7.62mm M60

^ weight unladen
# inside/outside width at tires.
* Overall dimensions listed in inches.

ENGINE DATA

ENGINE MAKE/MODEL	Chrysler 75M
NUMBER OF CYLINDERS	8
CUBIC INCH DISPLACEMENT	361
HORSEPOWER	191 @ 4000
TORQUE	325 @ 2400

The Cadillac Gage V-100 was standardized for US Forces as XM706 in 1964, after field evaluations of pilot models. This early production vehicle is seen in July of 1965 and differs from later production vehicles with flat panel hatches over the drivers' positions and angular cutouts for the wheel well openings.

A later production M706 of the 4th Division Military Police arrives at Camp Schmidt near Pleiku, Vietnam on 10 January 1970. Two M73 7.62mm machine guns are mounted in the turret, protected by their canvas foul-weather covers. The single vision block forward of the side door identifies this as a late production vehicle. (*National Archives*)

A 'Commando' armored car of the 57th Transport Battalion prepares to escort a convoy from the South Tank Farm and Fuel point of the 226th Service and Supply company near Chu Lai, Vietnam on 14 September 1970. The M706 was the perfect vehicle for the escort of truck convoys but were always in short supply. (*National Archives*)

Military Policemen, members of Company A, 720th Military Police Battalion, 18th MP Brigade, take a break while escorting a convoy near Chu Chi, Republic of Vietnam, in mid-August 1967. The two vision blocks forward of the left-side door identifies this as an early production vehicle. (*National Archives*)

A turretless version of the V-100 Commando was standardized for production for the US Air Force to provide perimeter security at air bases. The superstructure of the vehicle was topped with an armored parapet with folding doors. Designated XM706E2, the vehicle could mount a wide array of light weapons. Here a line of newly manufactured vehicles are seen outside the Cadillac Gage plant in Detroit, Michigan. (*National Museum of the United States Air Force*)

A pair of XM706E2 armored cars (the rear of the second vehicle to the extreme right) patrol perimeter roads on an Air Base in Southeast Asia. The fact that no weapons are visible and the crewmen wear no helmets points to a rather low threat level. The fuselage of a C-47 and other derelict aircraft line the road. *(National Museum of the United States Air Force)*

An XM706E2 passes a C-130 Hercules cargo aircraft on the tarmac of an airbase in Southeast Asia. The open top of the XM706E2 afforded the crew with better visibility than the standard turreted model, while sacrificing a bit of overhead protection. Note the two vision blocks on the hull side forward of the right-side door. *(National Museum of the United States Air Force)*

The US Air Force XM706E2 armored cars often received camouflage paint schemes with three colors similar to their aircraft in Vietnam. The pintle for mounting a weapon is visible on the rear parapet wall. The headlight guards were fitted with wire mesh to protect the lights from rock damage. (*TACOM LCMC History Office*)

Track Laying Vehicles

M76 Otter G-245

Developed in the late 1940s by the Pontiac Motor Division of General Motors, the M76 Otter was designed to provide the military with a lightweight amphibious carrier with a higher load capacity than the M29 Weasel. The vehicle was initially tested by the Army, eventually choosing to go another route, but it caught the interest of the US Marine Corps.

With a totally enclosed, insulated aluminum body, the Otter could carry eight passengers plus the two-man crew, or 3,000-pounds of cargo. The vehicle had hatches in the roof, and a pair of doors at the rear of the cargo/passenger area for loading and unloading. Two doors on either side of the cab were provided for the crew. A propeller was mounted at the rear below the pintle hook for use in the water. The location of the externally mounted fuel tanks and external stowage varied during the production run. Early vehicles had them mounted centered on the hull side, and to the rear of the hull sides on late models. A 5,000-pound capacity winch was mounted in the rear compartment under a seat.

The 3rd Motor Transport Battalion, 1st Marine Division Fleet Logistics Support Command, 1st Marine Brigade arrived in Da Nang with thirty-three Otters. This was their first deployment in Vietnam in 1965.

GENERAL DATA

MODEL	M76
WEIGHT^	12162
MAX TOWED LOAD	6000
LENGTH*	188
WIDTH*	98
HEIGHT*	108
STD TRACK WIDTH	30
MAX SPEED LAND WATER	28 4.5
FUEL CAPY	70
RANGE LAND	160
ELECTRICAL	24 negative
TRANSMISSION SPEEDS	2
TURNING RADIUS FEET	PIVOT

* Overall dimensions listed in inches.

^ Fighting weight

ENGINE DATA

ENGINE MAKE/MODEL*	Continental AOI-268-3A
NUMBER OF CYLINDERS	4 Opposed
CUBIC INCH DISPLACEMENT	269
HORSEPOWER	127 @ 3200
TORQUE	225 @ 2600
GOVERNED SPEED (rpm)	3200

The M76 Otter began development in the late 1940s as a replacement for the M29 Weasel. It was a small vehicle built almost entirely from aluminum. Its 30 inch wide tracks and pneumatic paired road wheels helped with its amphibious ability and flotation on soft ground. Power was provided by a Continental air-cooled AOI-268 horizontally opposed four-cylinder engine creating 130 horsepower. (*US Army photo*)

The M76 was adopted by the Marines in the mid-1950s and was deployed in relatively small numbers. Here two USMC M76s are offloaded from a landing craft at the Dong Ha docks in 1968. The lead vehicle is decorated with a menacing cartoon face on its bow. (*USMC*)

A Marine performs lubrication maintenance to the suspension of an M76 Otter on an improvised service lift supported by ammunition crates at Camp Big John outpost. The 1st Marine Regiment was using the M76 to provide resupply and medical evacuation to patrols west of Cua Viet in late June of 1968. (*USMC*)

A Marine crewman of an M76 Otter awaits assistance while crossing a river south of Cau Lu on 28 January 1969. The M76 could carry up to 3,000 pounds of cargo, almost equal to its own weight. (*National Archives*)

The M116 Husky G-299

The M116 Husky was designed by the Pacific Car and Foundry Company as part of various attempts to replace the M29 Weasel. Pacific built four pilot models, and three preproduction pilots. The production contract was awarded to the Blaw-Knox Company to build 197 units. The vehicle had a load capacity of 1½ tons, and was powered by a Chevrolet gasoline V8 driven through a GM 'Hydramatic' automatic transmission.

The lightweight hull was constructed of aluminum topped with a fiberglass cab, which had hatches in its roof for the driver and co-driver. The engine was located behind the driver, with the cooling air coming from a grill in the roof, and exiting through a grill on the right side.

All Huskies were completely amphibious without special preparation and were propelled through the water by their tracks. A winch was mounted on the front of the vehicle. A hinged door in the rear of the hull provided access to the cargo area. The rear floor could be raised to provide a flat cargo space or lowered to provide seating. A canvas cargo cover and bows were provided, or a hard winter top could be mounted.

The XM733

An armored version of the M116 was developed and built by Pacific Car and Foundry as the XM733. It was open-topped, and had mounting points for a variety of weapons. The Marine Corps fielded 93 XM733 vehicles in Southeast Asia beginning in 1966.

GENERAL DATA

MODEL	**M116**
WEIGHT	10600
LENGTH*	188.1
WIDTH*	82.1
HEIGHT*	79.1
MAX SPEED LAND WATER	37 4.2
FUEL CAPY	65
RANGE LAND	300
ELECTRICAL	24 negative
TRANSMISSION SPEEDS	4F 1R
TURNING RADIUS FEET	8

* Overall dimensions listed in inches.

ENGINE DATA

ENGINE MAKE/MODEL*	**Chevrolet**
NUMBER OF CYLINDERS	V-8
CUBIC INCH DISPLACEMENT	283
HORSEPOWER	160 @ 4600
TORQUE	210 @ 2400
GOVERNED SPEED (rpm)	4600

The M116 Husky was developed as a replacement for both the M29 Weasel and M76 Otter, as a light amphibious cargo and personnel carrier for use on marginal terrain. While normally operated with a canvas tilt over the cargo area, the fiberglass enclosure seen here was developed for operation in colder climates. (*US Army photo*)

The amphibious abilities and flotation over soft ground of the M116 Husky were put to the test in Vietnam. This USMC M116 is entering a irrigation canal down a steep bank, in Vietnam in 1970, with an XM733 behind it. These vehicles are being used to assist local villagers with their harvest. (*USMC*)

Another of seven Huskies that were used by the 11th Motor Transport battalion to assist local farmers in March 1970. The crew has hung a stateside license plate on the bow of the vehicle along with a section of spare track. A shovel is stored in a bracket on the right side of the body ahead of the windshield. (*USMC*)

The XM733 Assault Vehicle, or Armored Husky was built on the chassis of the M116 for the Marine Corps in 1966. This vehicle was also deployed to Vietnam by the USMC and generally was armed with a single M2 .50 cal. machine gun. This proving ground photo shows a variety of weapons that could be carried. (*US Army photo*)

Marines of 2nd Battalion, 1st Marines, patrol a perimeter in an XM733 Assault Vehicle armed with a pair of M60 light machine guns. The vehicle offered a mix of armored protection against small-arms fire and amphibious capability. (*USMC*)

Marines patrol a sandy area in an XM733 Armored Husky armed with the more traditional M2 .50 cal. machine gun. The wide cleated track of the Husky made it able to climb river banks, cross rivers, or to negotiate soft terrain and mud, characteristics much appreciated in Vietnam. (*USMC*)

M56 Scorpion G-289

Cadillac began production of 325 M56 Scorpion Self-Propelled Anti-Tank (SPAT) guns in 1957 at their Cleveland defense products plant. Known as the Scorpion, with its crew of four, and armed with a 90mm gun, the M56 was designed for the role of air-mobile anti-tank weapon. Scorpion had a top speed of 28 mph, powered by a Continental six-cylinder horizontally-opposed gasoline engine developing 200 horsepower, and a range of 140 miles.

Designed to be extremely lightweight the design of the M56 provided no weather protection for its four-man crew. The driver's station and controls were to the left of the main gun, with a windshield incorporated in the gun splinter shield. The radio equipment was to the driver's left, forming the base of the commander's seat. Two additional crew members rode on the other side of the gun breech.

The hull of the M56 was constructed completely of aluminum, the splinter shield being the only armor on the vehicle.

The ammunition for the 90mm M54 gun could be of AP-T, APC-T, HEAT, HEAT-T, HEP-T, WP, TP-T, HVAP-T or HVTP-T types. When firing, the gun was served by the gunlayer and driver from their positions on the vehicle, while the rest of the gun crew was on the ground. The gun was manually elevated and traversed. The vehicle carried an ammunition load of twenty-nine rounds.

The road wheels of M56 featured pneumatic tires, unusual for a track laying vehicle. The Scorpion was in use by the 82nd and 101st Airborne Divisions from 1957 until 1970, including service in Vietnam. South Korea, Spain and Morocco also acquired a few units. The M56 was deemed too light for its gun; when fired the recoil would lift the front of the vehicle off the ground and the muzzle blast would kick up huge amounts of dust, revealing its position.

GENERAL DATA

MODEL	M56
WEIGHT^	15500
LENGTH*	230
WIDTH*	101.5
HEIGHT*	81
MAX SPEED	28 mph
FUEL CAPY	55 gallons
RANGE	140 miles
ELECTRICAL	24 volt
TRANSMISSION SPEEDS	2
TURNING RADIUS FEET	9

* Overall dimensions listed in inches. Measure with main gun facing forward.

^ Fighting weight.

ENGINE DATA

ENGINE MAKE/MODEL*	**Continental AOI-402-5**
NUMBER OF CYLINDERS	6 Opposed
CUBIC INCH DISPLACEMENT	402
HORSEPOWER	200 @ 3000
TORQUE	355 @ 2750

The 90mm Full-tracked, Self-propelled Gun M56, sometimes referred to as a SPAT, was nicknamed the Scorpion. The pilot vehicles had muzzle brakes on the 90mm gun; the production M56s such as this one, registration number 40232479, replaced the muzzle brake with a blast deflector with round holes on the sides. Production of the vehicles was undertaken at the Cleveland Tank Plant. (*National Archives*)

The crew of four comprised the driver, gunner, loader, and vehicle commander. A blast shield with a window on the left side for the driver was on the gun mount. Power was provided by a Continental AOI-402-5 air-cooled gasoline engine through an Allison CD-150-4 transmission. (*National Archives*)

The M56 Scorpion SPAT was briefly fielded in Vietnam. This example is with Co. D, 16th Armor of the 173rd Airborne Brigade at Bien Hoa 10 June 1965. (*National Archives via Steve Zaloga*)

M50 Ontos G-288

In November 1950 the farm machinery division of Allis-Chalmers began work designing the M50 as a powerful, airborne tank destroyer. The basic requirements of the vehicle were set: it was to use the six-cylinder GMC 302 which was in use in the new M135 and M211 trucks, coupled to an Allison cross-drive transmission, and its weight and size must allow it to be carried within the cargo aircraft of the day. A team at times numbering fifty engineers completed initial design work within two weeks. A portion of the Allis-Chalmers plant in LaPorte, Indiana was closed off with a wall to ensure the confidential classification of the project, where prototypes were assembled. Test runs of the vehicles were done on weekends when the remainder of the facility was closed. Prototypes T165E1 and T165E2 underwent tests, and the vehicle was standardized as the Rifle, Self-Propelled, Full Tracked, Multiple 106mm, M50. A contract was issued to Allis-Chalmers on 12 August 1955 to produce the vehicle. Only 297 of the original 1,000 planned for production were completed when production ceased in 1957, and the Army rejected the entire series. The US Marine Corps was interested in the vehicle and took delivery of all vehicles produced, by this time known as Ontos.

The vehicle was armed with six 106mm M40 recoilless rifles, which naturally could only be reloaded from outside the vehicle. Four of the M40s were fitted with .50 caliber spotting rifles, which were used to ensure that the main rounds hit the intended target. As built a M1919A4 .30 caliber machine gun was installed for self-defense use. Provision was included for stowage of eighteen main gun rounds.

The original engine was replaced in 176 vehicles with a Chrysler 361 cubic inch gasoline V8 beginning in 1963. The resulting repowered vehicle was re-designated M50A1. The new engine required new engine compartment doors with cooling louvers that extended forward past the travel lock.

The Ontos was among the first USMC armor to land in the Republic of Vietnam on 8 March 1965 with the 3rd Platoon, Company C, 3rd Antitank Battalion. By the end of 1965 roughly sixty-five vehicles were in service with Marine units in Vietnam.

GENERAL DATA

MODEL	M50
WEIGHT^	19050
LENGTH*	150.75
WIDTH*	102.25
HEIGHT*	83.875
MAX SPEED	30 mph
FUEL CAPY	47 gallons
RANGE	150 miles
ELECTRICAL	24 volt
TRANSMISSION SPEEDS	5
TURNING RADIUS FEET	pivot

* Overall dimensions listed in inches.

^ Fighting weight.

ENGINE DATA

ENGINE MAKE/MODEL*	GMC 302	Chrysler 75M
NUMBER OF CYLINDERS	6	8
CUBIC INCH DISPLACEMENT	301.6	361
HORSEPOWER	127 @ 3350	191 @ 4000
TORQUE	254 @ 1800	325 @ 2400

The M50 multiple self-propelled recoilless rifle was obsolete for its designed air-transportable anti-tank role by the time it first saw combat in Vietnam. It served instead as a fire-support or static-defense weapon, or as a reconnaissance vehicle. Its ungainly appearance inspired the name 'Ontos', which in ancient Greek means 'thing'.(*USMC*)

The M50 was equipped with six 106mm recoilless rifles mounted on a small turret with limited traverse and elevation. The crew of three, commander, loader and driver, loaded the weapons from the exterior of the small vehicle. Production of the vehicles began in 1952, and used the same 302 cubic inch gasoline engine then used in the GMC M135 2½ ton truck. (*USMC*)

An M50A1 of G Company, 2nd Battalion, 3rd Marine Division moves onto a road near Cam Lo, South Vietnam, during November 1968. A length of spare track is carried on the bow of the vehicle's hull. The Ontos weighed less than 10 tons, and with its wide track and powerful engine proved very maneuverable with a speed of up to 30 mph (48 kph). (*USMC*)

The external mounting of the recoilless rifles on the M50A1 made them vulnerable to the elements. Here a crew of an Ontos clean the weapons after traversing a muddy road, 3 November 1967. A pioneer tool rack and the engine exhaust is visible on the right side of the hull below the rifles. (*USMC*)

M548 G-403

The M548 was built using automotive components of the M113A1 family of vehicles. It was developed by FMC to meet a Signal Corps requirement for a carrier for the AN/MPQ-32 counter-battery radar system but was not used for this original mission. The vehicles were used in a variety of roles, including ammunition carrier for the M107, M108, M109, and M110 self-propelled artillery pieces.

GENERAL DATA

MODEL	M548A1
WEIGHT^	28300
LENGTH*	232
WIDTH*	105.75
HEIGHT*	110.75
MAX SPEED	35 mph
FUEL CAPY	105 gallons
RANGE LAND	300
ELECTRICAL	24 negative
TRANSMISSION SPEEDS	3
TURNING RADIUS FEET	14

* Overall dimensions listed in inches.

^ Fighting weight

ENGINE DATA

ENGINE MAKE/MODEL*	6V53
NUMBER OF CYLINDERS	V-6
CUBIC INCH DISPLACEMENT	318
HORSEPOWER	212 @ 2800
TORQUE	492 @ 1300

The M548 was developed as an unarmored cargo-carrying variant of the M113. It shared its suspension, tracks, Detroit Diesel engine and drive train. The vehicle has a payload capacity of 5 tons, and speed on roads of 38 mph. The height of the vehicle can be reduced by removing the canvas cargo cover and folding the windscreen, allowing it to be transported in a C-130 cargo aircraft.

Members of Troop E, 11th Armored Cavalry prepare night defensive positions near Memut, Cambodia, 4 May 1970. The M548 was often used to carry provisions and ammunition for combat units. M113s and M109 self-propelled howitzers ring the perimeter of the area in the background.

M114 G-300

The M114 was developed as a reconnaissance vehicle for armored cavalry units. It was prevented from being successful in this role by its poor cross-country performance. The major design flaw was that its hull extended forward of the tracks, causing it to hang when attempting to cross ditches.

The M114 was lightweight and air transportable, its hull constructed of welded 5083 aluminum alloy. It was fully amphibious, with water propulsion provided by its shrouded tracks. The small interior had little room for the three-man crew of a driver, commander, observer and a single passenger.

The M114 was powered by a Chevrolet 283 V8 engine driven through a 305MC 'Hydramatic' transmission. The suspension consisted of four road wheels on each side attached to swing arms on torsion bars. Front-mounted drive sprockets drove band-type tracks, with tension controlled by idler wheels at the rear.

The commander had a cupola with an externally mounted .50 caliber machine gun on early production models. Later vehicles had the machine gun enclosed within a turret. The commander's hatch was on the left side of the hull roof, directly behind the driver's hatch. The observer's hatch was on the right hull side, just to the rear of the commander's position. Two pedestal mounts for a .30 caliber machine gun were provided at the observer's position. The .30 cal. was replaced with a 7.62mm M60 machine gun early in the vehicle's production. A large circular door was in the rear of the hull.

T114 was the classification for the first 615 vehicles produced in 1962. For the later vehicles with the turret-type machine gun mount added to the next 600 units, the classification changed to T114E1. These were reclassified as M114 and M114A1 respectively in 1963, with an additional 2,495 M114A1s produced in 1963 and 1964.

The M114 series was built by Cadillac and Chrysler, both at Cleveland Tank Plant, but under different contracts. Cadillac produced the vehicles from 1962 until Chrysler was awarded a contract for production in the same government-owned, contractor-operated facility on 4 December 1963. Elsewhere in the same vast building, General Motors continued building M551s. Chrysler delivered their first M114A1 on 15 January 1965. In 1965, the contract was re-bid, and control of the Cleveland Tank Plant in its entirety reverted to General Motors, who continued production of the M114A1.

The intended weapon for the turret of the M114A1 was the 20mm gun M139, which was still under development when the T114E1s and M114A1s were produced, the vehicles receiving the .50 caliber machine gun in their place. Some were fitted to M114s and M114A1s when the weapon became available, the vehicles then being reclassified as M114E2 and M114A1E1.

In 1962 eighty of the M114s were supplied to the ARVN who organized the vehicles into four armored cavalry squadrons, with a few being delivered to the ARVN armor school and technical service installations. These deliveries continued into 1963. As with the other new US-produced equipment being fielded in Vietnam, performance of the M114 was closely watched by US observers, whose 28 September 1963 evaluations noted:

(1) 'The M114s frequently mired down in areas which the M113s negotiated without difficulty.'
(2) 'It should be noted here that the M113s usually become stuck as a result of trying to retrieve the M114s. The M114s had difficulty in keeping up with the M113s everywhere except on hard-surfaced roads.'
(3) 'The M114 reduces the speed of cross country maneuverability of the M113 troop.'

(4) 'The troop commander has used the M114 on a trial basis for approximately three months. He is dissatisfied with it in that it cannot keep up with the M113 during cross-country marches. He feels that it is underpowered, shifts down to its low gears too quickly, and is extremely rough riding. He also mentioned that the travel lock for the .50 caliber machine gun will disengage when the vehicle hits certain angles.'

Not surprisingly, in November 1964 the use of the M114 in Vietnam was discontinued.

GENERAL DATA

MODEL	M114
WEIGHT^	14749
LENGTH*	175.75
WIDTH*	91.75
HEIGHT*	91.125
MAX SPEED	40 mph
FUEL CAPY	110 gallons
RANGE LAND	300 miles
ELECTRICAL	24 volt
TRANSMISSION SPEEDS	3
TURNING RADIUS FEET	32

* Overall dimensions listed in inches.
^ Fighting weight

ENGINE DATA

ENGINE MAKE/MODEL*	Chevrolet
NUMBER OF CYLINDERS	V-8
CUBIC INCH DISPLACEMENT	283
HORSEPOWER	160 @ 4600
TORQUE	210 @ 2400
GOVERNED SPEED (rpm)	4600

This M114 Command and Reconnaissance Vehicle was photographed while undergoing testing at Fort Knox, Kentucky. (*TACOM LCMC History Office*)

When equipped with a turret-mounted 20mm gun, the vehicle was designated M114A1. (*TACOM LCMC History Office*)

M113 G-294

Experience with open-top half-track personnel carriers in WWII made clear the need for a fully-enclosed armored personnel carrier. The M75 was the first such vehicle successfully used by US troops, with its combat debut coming in Korea in 1953. The cost of the vehicle was extremely high, in large part due to its use of parts common to the M41 light tank. Because of this high cost, the Army sought to develop a lower-cost option and also wanted a vehicle that would retain the positive characteristics of the M75, but weigh less in order to be airmobile. The M113 APC was developed from these parameters and was standardized in April 1959.

Production of the vehicle began at FMC Corporation in 1960, and the M113 and its updated successors served as the standard armored personnel carrier of the US Army until the advent of the Bradley Fighting Vehicle decades later. While now only in limited use by US armed forces, the M113 remains in service in many other nations around the world.

The M113 was never given an official name, but was known by its crews as 'one-one-threes', or 'tracks'. Both gasoline powered M113s and diesel M113A1s served in numerous roles in Vietnam. The vehicles shuttled troops forward to battle, or served to evacuate wounded. The aluminum construction made the M113 vulnerable to mines, and troops are often seen riding on the exterior, and the floors of the troop compartment lined with sand bags for added protection. The roof plates often mounted improvised machine gun mounts and kits were developed to add armor protection to these mounts and to the commander's cupola. The rear of the vehicle was dominated by a hydraulically operated ramp for exiting the troop compartment. A smaller door was also mounted within the ramp for entry and exit.

The driver's position was on the front left, and to his right was the power plant. The driver hatch was surrounded with four M17 periscopes, and the hatch had a mounting for a M19 infrared periscope as well. The commander's station is behind the driver and his cupola was mounted on the centerline of the vehicle. The cupola was equipped with five M17 periscopes and a pintle mount for an M2 .50 cal. machine gun. The troop area had provisions for carrying eleven passengers.

The M113 had five road wheels per side, with drive sprockets at the front and hydraulically controlled idlers at the rear. There were no track return rollers. The M113 was amphibious and was propelled in the water by its tracks. This feature was seldom used due to limited freeboard when the vehicle was in the water.

A Chrysler 75M V8 gasoline engine powered the initial production of M113, driving through an Allison TX200-2 transmission. Soon after the initial production contracts for the M113 were awarded work began on a diesel-powered version. A diesel version powered by the General Motors 6V53 V6 engine was standardized as the M113A1 in May 1963. Power was transmitted through an Allison TX-100 automatic transmission and a DS-200 controlled differential. Priority was given to equipping units in Vietnam with the Diesel M113A1 variant with increased crew survivability due to its less volatile fuel. All M113s in Vietnam were Diesel-powered vehicles by July of 1968.

GENERAL DATA

MODEL	**M113**	**M113A1**
WEIGHT^	20160	20870
MAX TOWED LOAD	22900	24080
LENGTH*	191.5	191.5
WIDTH*	105.75	105.75
HEIGHT*	98.25	98.25
STD TRACK WIDTH	15	15
MAX SPEED	40 mph	40 mph
FUEL CAPY	80 gallons	95 gallons
RANGE LAND	200 miles	300 miles
ELECTRICAL	24 volt	24 volt
TRANSMISSION SPEEDS	2	2
TURNING RADIUS FEET	12′ 7″	12′ 7″

* Overall dimensions listed in inches.
^ Fighting weight

ENGINE DATA

ENGINE MAKE/MODEL*	**Chrysler A-710-B**	**Detroit Diesel 6V53**
NUMBER OF CYLINDERS	V-8	V-6
CUBIC INCH DISPLACEMENT	361	318
HORSEPOWER	215 @ 4000	212 @ 2800
TORQUE	332 @ 2800	492 @ 1300

This M113 retains its factory installed track shrouds, or sand shields. These shrouds interfered with maintenance of the tracks and suspension and were often discarded in combat use in Vietnam. The vehicle is equipped with the ACAV gun shield kit and has the heavy lifting or towing eyes present on the glacis of some early model M113s. (*Rock Island Arsenal*)

Members of Troop B, 1st Battalion, 4th Cavalry, ride the roof of an M113 on patrol near Saigon in October 1965. Mines were a constant threat to vehicles in Vietnam; riding on the roof gave troops one more layer of armored protection against their blasts. This vehicle is equipped with an early attempt to protect the gun position on the commander's cupola with added vertical armor plating. (*National Archives*)

This ACAV-equipped M113 is the commanding officer's vehicle of the 11th Forward Headquarters at Bien Hoa. The rear ramp door is lowered, providing a view of the lived-in appearance of the vehicle's interior, crammed with the crew's personal belongings such as an Igloo cooler, buckets, bed rolls and cans. Another ACAV M113 is seen in the background. (*Chris Harlow*)

An M113 bearing the Red Cross markings of an ambulance emerges from a muddy field to cross an irrigation canal. The APC is operating in tandem with a second M113 attached to the rear by push bars, a technique often used to cross soft or difficult terrain. This vehicle is a part of the 60th Infantry Regiment seen on 24 March 1967. (*National Archives*)

The M113A1 porta-bridge had a number of names including lightweight assault bridge and marginal terrain bridge. The bridge when fully extended spanned 33 feet and supported a weight of 15 tons. The extra 2,700-pound weight of the device added stress on the front suspension and caused premature wear to torsion bars and other suspension components. (*Ordnance Museum*)

An M113A1 with the lightweight folding assault bridge in the stowed position prepares to tow an M113 ACAV. These vehicles belong to Troop A, 3rd Squadron, 4th Cavalry Regiment in South Vietnam, 3 August 1969. The roll of cyclone fencing on the trim vane of the rear vehicle was used for perimeter defense against anti-tank rockets when in a static position. (*National Archives*)

The same vehicle is seen from the opposite side as it proceeds toward a rubber plantation following a reconnaissance patrol along Highway 23 in South Vietnam. The folding assault bridge could be set in place, controlled from within the protection of the vehicle's armor, in only two minutes. (*National Archives*)

This M113 of the 919th Combat Engineer Company, 11th Armored Cavalry Regiment clears a road of mines near Long Giao, South Vietnam, November 1968. The mine roller device attached to the glacis of the APC, allowing the weight of the rollers to safely explode mines ahead of the vehicle. The area is believed to be clear of mines or the driver would be operating within the protection of the vehicle. No machine gun mount or shield is visible on the commander's cupola. (*National Archives*)

The M163A1 Vulcan mounted the M168 20mm cannon in an open turret on the chassis of the M113A1. The M168 Vulcan Air Defense System was a six-barreled rotary weapon capable of firing 3,000 rounds per minute and was designed for defense against low flying aircraft. In the Vietnam war these vehicles were deployed in anti-personnel missions. (*TACOM LCMC History Office*)

This M163A1 has turned off of Highway 13 while on convoy protection duty to fire at enemy positions along the tree line on 15 January 1969. The vehicle is equipped with additional flotation cells on the bow trim vane and along each side to maintain its amphibious capability with the added weight of the weapon system. (*National Archives*)

The M577 was a variant of the M113 developed to carry additional command radios with a raised roof section over the troop area to allow standing within the vehicle. The prototype XM577s were converted from M113s and lack the armored protection for the diesel generator and had the additional lifting eyes on the outside edge of the glacis. (*TACOM LCMC History Office*)

The M577 was equipped with a tarpaulin 'annex' or tent that could be erected and attached to the rear of the vehicle with the rear ramp up or down. The tent provided significant additional working room for command troops with rudimentary protection from the elements while working in a static location. (*Kevin Emdee collection*)

A column of ACAV-equipped M113s follows an M577A1 through an MP checkpoint on the road between Fire Base Dakota and Di An, South Vietnam, in early March 1970. The soldiers from 1st Battalion (Mechanized), 2nd Brigade, 16th Infantry Regiment ride on the roof of the command-post carrier for additional protection from mines. (*National Archives*)

Troops of 52nd Artillery Group prepare to deploy an M577A1 as a fire-directional vehicle at Fire Base Exodus during late June of 1970. The vehicle has been towed into position across muddy terrain, depositing a heavy layer of mud on the front of the vehicle. Note that the driver's hatch has been left open while towing the vehicle. (*TACOM LCMC History Office*)

Two M577s are deployed with their tents set up between them. These vehicles are serving as the command post for C Troop, 1st Squadron, 11th Cavalry Regiment during Operation Junction City, on 3 March 1967. The tent annexes are attached at their large side doors and the other end to the rear of the vehicles, supported by a tubular framework that was carried on the roof of the vehicle when not in use. (Kevin Emdee collection)

The M106 107mm Mortar Carrier was developed to mount the mortar within the troop area of the vehicle to be fired through doors in the roof. The mortar base plate is mounted on the left side of this M106A2, and the rotator assembly on the right rear mudguard. This allowed the mortar to be dismounted and fired conventionally outside the vehicle. (*TACOM LCMC History Office*)

This posed photograph of the XM106 prototype shows the general layout of the interior through the open rear troop ramp. The internal stowage of the vehicle was modified from that of the M113 to allow eigty-eight mortar rounds to be carried within the protection of the armor. The empty ammunition racks are visible on the right internal hull wall. (*Kevin Emdee collection*)

LVTP-5

The LVTP-5 was designed as a replacement for the WWII-era LVTs. The development of the vehicle took place in 1951, production beginning in August 1952 by the Ingersoll Products Division of Borg-Warner. At over 30 feet in length, the LVTP-5 was much larger than its predecessors. The front of the hull was of an inverted-V shape, which greatly improved in-water performance. The tracks were mounted low on the hull of the LVTP-5 much like a tank rather than the all-round track design used previously on the LVTs. There was an internal return channel for the upper return run of track. The V-shaped bow formed a ramp which was lowered for loading and unloading cargo or troops. Up to thirty-four infantry troops (twenty-five for water operation) could be carried. A large hatch and two smaller ones in the roof of the passenger compartment provided alternate means of loading and unloading the vehicle. The crew and passenger compartment made up most of the front of the interior. The driver's position was at the front of the vehicle above the left track channel. On the right side was the vehicle commander's position. A machine gun cupola could be installed at the front of the vehicle's roof between the driver's and commander's hatches. Two small roof hatches at the rear of the vehicle provided access to the engine compartment.

Inverted grousers in the inner face of the LVTP-5 tracks aided the propulsion of the vehicle while it was in water. The grousers also served as center guide teeth for the track, running between the paired road wheels. The LVTP-5 used thirty-six road wheels per side, one wheel of each pair was of conventional design, with a solid rubber tire mounted on a metal wheel to bear the weight of the vehicle. The outer steel-rimmed wheel absorbed shock and heavy loads.

Lessons learned in the field brought about improvements to the engine air intake and exhaust system. The new improved vehicles received the classification of LVTP-5A1. The two models can be differentiated externally by the A1's large housing on the vehicle's rear roof above the engine.

GENERAL DATA

MODEL	LVTP-5
WEIGHT^	87780
LENGTH*	356
WIDTH*	140.5
HEIGHT*	103
MAX SPEED LAND WATER	30 6.8
FUEL CAPY	456
RANGE	190

* Overall dimensions listed in inches. Measure with main gun facing forward, and anti-aircraft machine gun mounted.

ENGINE DATA

ENGINE MAKE/MODEL*	**Continental LV-1790-1**
NUMBER OF CYLINDERS	12 90 Degree V
CUBIC INCH DISPLACEMENT	1790
HORSEPOWER	704 @ 2800
TORQUE	1440 @ 2000

The bow of an LVTP-5 is seen here in the Saint Louis Car Company factory. At nearly 30 feet long, 12 feet wide and weighing in at 37 tons, the LVTP-5 was a massive vehicle capable of carrying up to thirty-four armed troops. First accepted into service for US Forces in 1956, over 1,100 were produced. (*Washington University*)

The same LVTP-5, now with the forward ramp in the lowered position, is seen at the factory in St Louis, Missouri. The ramp was electrically powered through cables with an emergency manual operation. The roof was fitted with a number of hatches, some seen here in the open position, that could also be used for exiting the vehicle while in the water. (*Washington University*)

Marines of the 3rd Division disembark from LVTP-5s at Da Nang in Vietnam, on 12 April 1965. The troop ramp makes up the majority of the front of the vehicle. The only armament carried by the vehicle is a single .30 cal. light machine gun mounted in a rotating cupola on the right front roof. (*National Archives*)

Marines take a break outside of a pair of LVTP-5s in South Vietnam during 1965. The terrain of Vietnam was not well suited for the LVTP-5, which was not designed for extended use inland or over uneven ground. The fuel tank was mounted in the floor and was susceptible to mine damage. The M113 was much preferred as a troop carrier in the conflict. (*National Archives*)

The same two LVTP-5s are seen with the Marines now in full gear preparing to move off on a patrol away from the vehicles. The Continental LV-1790-1 V-12 gasoline engine of the LVTP-5 produced more than 700 horsepower gave the vehicle adequate speed over even ground and in the water. The weight of the vehicle and the design of the suspension limited its mobility over rough or soft surfaces. (*National Archives*)

M42 Duster

By 1951, the Army realized the need for a replacement for the M19 gun motor carriage, then the Army's standard self-propelled 40mm antiaircraft gun. Development began that year, resulting in the M42, which shared many common mechanical components with the M41 Light Tank.

The pilot vehicle, designated T141, was delivered by Cadillac Motor Car Division of General Motors in August 1951. In common with the T41, prototype of the M41 Light Tank, were the rear of the hull, and its power train, including the Continental AOS-895-3 air-cooled engine and Allison CD-500-3 cross drive transmission, and the suspension.

American Car and Foundry (ACF Industries) joined Cadillac in production of the vehicles in April 1952, once accepted by the military. Although production had begun by both manufacturers in 1952, the vehicle was not type classified as Standard and designated M42 until October 1953. By this time the vehicle was already known as 'Duster'.

The M42 was armed with dual automatic Bofors M2A1 40mm anti-aircraft cannon as on the WWII-designed M19. Early production vehicles were equipped with conical flash suppressors on the gun muzzles, similar to those used on the 40mm weapons in naval service. Later production vehicles had two styles of three-prong flash suppressors.

Early production M42s had two doors between the driver's and commander's hatches on the upper surface of the hulls. Their intent was to allow ammunition cans to be passed from the hull to the turret. These doors were eliminated on later vehicles.

A pintle for a light machine gun was attached to the side armor of the rotating 40mm mount. Upgrades that the Duster received during its service life included updated communications equipment, and the replacement of the carbureted engine with a fuel-injected version yielding improved performance and range. The fuel-injected vehicles were classified as M42A1.

Although the M42 was deployed stateside and in many locations globally, it was considered by many to be obsolete and unable to support ground troops against modern jet aircraft and helicopters. Most M42s were relegated to National Guard units of various states. However, three Duster Battalions were deployed between 1966 and 1971 as US involvement in Vietnam escalated. The 1st Bn 44th ADA was the first to arrive; it was deployed in the north and was attached to the 3rd Marine Regiment (ICORP, IFFV).

The 5th Bn 2nd ADA followed and was deployed in the south (III CORP, IIFFV). The final unit arriving was the 4th Bn 60th ADA and deployed in the

Central Highlands (IICORP, IFFV). The Dusters were typically deployed in pairs with four vehicles comprising a section. Two sections (1st and 2nd) comprised a platoon of eight and two platoons (1st and 2nd) comprised the battery of sixteen Dusters. There were four batteries (A, B, C, and D), plus spare vehicles held under the commanding Headquarters battery. These units proved very successful, not in their intended anti-aircraft role, but in supporting troops against ground targets.

GENERAL DATA

MODEL	M42	M42A1
WEIGHT^	49500	49500
MAX TOWED LOAD	5000	5000
LENGTH*	250.25	250.25
WIDTH*	126 15/16	126 15/16
HEIGHT*	112.125	112.125
TRACK WIDTH	21	21
MAX SPEED	45	45
FUEL CAPY	80	80
RANGE	100	100
ELECTRICAL	24 negative	24 negative
TRANSMISSION SPEEDS	2	2
TURNING RADIUS FEET	PIVOT	PIVOT

* Overall dimensions listed in inches. Guns facing forward.

^ Fighting weight.

ENGINE DATA

VEHICLE MODEL	M42	M42A1
ENGINE MAKE/MODEL	AOS-895-3	AOSI-895-5
NUMBER OF CYLINDERS	Opposed 6	Opposed 6
CUBIC INCH DISPLACEMENT	895.9	895.9
HORSEPOWER	500 @ 2800	500 @ 2800
TORQUE	955 @ 2400	955 @ 2400
GOVERNED SPEED (rpm)	2800	2800

The M42 Duster went into production in 1952 and was developed for protection of ground troops from low-flying aircraft. It shared the suspension, lower hull, track and automotive components with the M41 Light Tank. The twin 40mm anti-aircraft guns were capable of firing 150 rounds per minute each. The vehicles proved very effective against ground targets in the Vietnam War. (*Patton Museum*)

An M42 Duster of 1st Battalion, 44th Artillery (Automatic Weapon, Self-Propelled), I Field Force Vietnam, disembarks from a landing craft after a river crossing. An antenna matching unit is mounted below the antenna on the right-side gun-shield. The gun barrels are equipped with three-prong flash suppressors. (*National Archives*)

The M42's original Continental AOS-395-5 engine was replaced by the fuel-injected Continental AOSI-895-5 engine, resulting in the M42A1. This M42A1 belongs to 4th Battalion, 60th Artillery operating in the Dak To province in July 1967. An M60 light machine gun is mounted to the right side of the turret and the ring sights are visible on both sides of the gun. Square T141-style mudguards are mounted to this vehicle's fenders. (*National Archives*)

The motor pool of Alpha Battery, 5th Battalion, 2nd Artillery performs maintenance on 6 M42 Dusters in 1970 or 1971. The right-side machine gun mount on the left front vehicle is equipped with an ACAV style shield. A power pack for a Duster is on the ground beside the 2½ ton 6X6 truck. None of the 40mm guns appears to be mounted with flash suppressors. (*Jack Ryan via NDQSA*)

M551 Sheridan G-310

Named for Civil War Union General Philip Sheridan, the M551 Sheridan was a controversial vehicle almost from the time production began. Many saw the Sheridan as an overly complex and expensive weapons system that was minimally effective. Others view the Sheridan as a vehicle that in spite of initial problems and expense, delivered capabilities that were not only unequalled, but which have been lacking in the US military since its retirement from combat units in 1996.

In 1957 the Soviet Union was outfitting its forces with a new light tank – but theirs was amphibious. The US Army was then challenged by a Congressional committee looking at military matters, why was the new light tank being proposed for production not also amphibious?

Development of the XM551 Armored Reconnaissance/Airborne Assault Vehicle was initiated in response to this challenge. The resultant vehicle looked like a tank, but officially, it was not a tank. As the name indicated, the XM551 was designed to be a light reconnaissance vehicle with both amphibious and airmobile capabilities.

The hull of the vehicle made of welded 7039 aluminum alloy armor plate. While this indeed helped achieve the desired light weight, when the vehicle first appeared in a combat environment, the aluminum hull was known to be extremely vulnerable to anti-tank mines. Because of prior experience with the M113, which also featured a welded aluminum hull, a hull armor kit was developed to be fitted to those vehicles that were sent to Vietnam.

The turret of the M551 housed three of the four-man vehicle crew, the commander, gunner and loader. Unlike the hull, the turret was constructed of welded armored steel castings. The driver's position was in the front center of the hull. To improve flotation, the aluminum hull was surrounded by a layer of high-density foam encased in an additional aluminum skin. Powering the vehicle was a six-cylinder Detroit Diesel engine.

Cadillac Division of General Motors was responsible for the vehicle's development; when production began responsibility for the project had been transferred to the Allison Division of General Motors. A total of 1,562 of the vehicles were produced in the Cleveland Tank Plant between 29 July 1966 and 1970.

The 152mm Gun/Launcher, the main armament for the M551, could fire either conventional ammunition or the Ford-produced Shillelagh anti-tank missile. While the weapon (which was common with the M60A2 Starship) was primarily intended as a missile launcher, its secondary gun role proved most troublesome and most widely used.

Most of the issues with the gun were actually ammunition-related. The Sheridan's ammunition had combustible cartridge cases rather than a conventional metal cartridge case. In theory, when the round was fired, the cartridge case was consumed by burning, with the ash expelled from the muzzle – thus solving the problem of handling and storing the used cartridge cases. These cases had to be protected from moisture and humidity to ensure that they would stay together and completely burn. Humidity was obviously a major problem in Vietnam. A removable bag system was developed to protect the round from moisture, the bag being removed just as the round was chambered. The fragile nature of the rounds also increased the vehicle's vulnerability to land mines. Striking a mine meant there was a real risk of ammunition detonation, thus many Sheridan crewmen rode outside the vehicle.

In Vietnam, where there was rarely tank-to-tank combat, a significant shortcoming in the weapon system was the lack of alternative ammunition, such as anti-personnel ammunition. To answer this, the M625 flechette anti-personnel round was rapidly developed while the Sheridan began to be considered for deployment.

So equipped, the Sheridan saw extensive use in Vietnam, where its light weight was a blessing in rice paddies, and a curse in thick jungle, where it simply could not crush its way through vegetation like a true tank.

GENERAL DATA

MODEL	**M551**
WEIGHT^	33460
LENGTH*	248.3
WIDTH*	110
HEIGHT*	150
CREW	4
MAX SPEED	45
FUEL CAPY	158
RANGE	350
ELECTRICAL	24 negative
TRANSMISSION SPEEDS	4F 2R
TURNING RADIUS FEET	PIVOT
ARMAMENT MAIN SECONDARY FLEXIBLE	1x 152mm 1x .30 cal. 1x .50 cal.

* Overall dimensions listed in inches. Measure with main gun facing forward and anti-aircraft machine gun mounted.

^ Fighting weight.

ENGINE DATA

ENGINE MAKE/MODEL*	**General Motors 6V53T**
NUMBER OF CYLINDERS	6
CUBIC INCH DISPLACEMENT	318.6
HORSEPOWER	300 @ 2800
TORQUE	615 @ 2100

The XM551 was equipped with the XM81 152mm gun-launcher, that fired a conventional round, or the XM13 Shillelagh Guided Missile. It was conceived originally as an amphibious, air-droppable Armored Reconnaissance/Airborne Assault Vehicle (AR/AAV). The production M551 mounted a Xenon searchlight, and the .50-caliber machine gun on the cupola had a small folding armored shield. (*Rock Island Arsenal Museum*)

Near Cu Chi on 12 February 1969, the M551 Sheridan 'HARD CORE 7' takes up a firing position along a sandy trail. The Xenon Searchlight is protected by a canvas cover. The cyclone fencing wire is strung along the bow of the vehicle as added protection against shaped charge weapons. A chess piece is painted on the rear portion of the gun tube, and the number 27 on the left sponson. (*National Archives*)

The crew of an M551 with Troop A, 3rd Squadron, 4th Cavalry take a break on the turret at Landing Zone 'Hampton', 3 August 1969. A red band is painted on the gun tube with the vehicle nickname 'Sudden Death' in white. The crew's personal belongings are stowed in an improvised rack on the turret rear, constructed from concrete-reinforcing rod and chain-link fence material. Smoke grenades are strung along the turret side in easy reach from the commander's cupola, and along the rear stowage rack. (*National Archives*)

The crew of 'Birth-Control', an M551 of the 11th Cavalry completes a sweep of enemy territory in 1970. The commander is holding a captured AK47 assault rifle, and the name 'Marcia' is painted on his machine gun shield in white. The vehicle has numerous bits of stowage lashed in various places around the hull and turret. Crates and boxes were often attached to the ACAV shields on the cupola. (*Doug Kibbey*)

Troop G, 11th Armored Cavalry Regiment resupply with food, fuel and ammunition in the Tan Uyen District, in February 1972. The M551 Sheridan has been fitted out to suit the needs of her crew, with an additional .50 cal. machine gun mount on the gunner's side of the turret roof and improvised stowage racks on the turret side. (*Doug Kibbey*)

M48 series vehicles G-254

The need to replace the M26 Pershing that began production late in WWII drove the development of the M48 Medium Tank. The Pershing was always considered to be underpowered using the same gasoline engine that had powered late production M4 Sherman Medium Tanks. Stop-gap measures were developed and went into production, including the M46, an M26 with a new powerful air-cooled twelve-cylinder Continental engine, and the M47, which mounted the new turret from the T42 program on a modified M46 hull. Chrysler began development of the new tank in 1950, and testing of pilot models began in February of 1953. The conflict in Korea proved the need for production of the replacement tanks. Even before standardization the T48 was approved for production, with nearly 1,000 produced. The production model was standardized as the '90mm gun tank M48'.

The M48 series went through modifications throughout the 1950s and 1960s', addressing issues that included its limited range and limited visibility from the commander's cupola to improving the fire control system.

The raised rear engine-deck that is a key feature of the post-M48A1 tanks came into being with the T48E2 project, which commenced in early 1954. This raised deck enclosed a radically new engine exhaust system with an insulated exhaust tunnel running over the engine and emitting the hot exhaust gases through two grille doors at the rear of the hull. This reduced the infrared signature of the tank, making it more difficult for an enemy to detect. The T48E2 was standardized as the Tank, 90mm Gun, M48A2 on 6 October 1955, and began production two months later. The M48A2 had numerous internal improvements, such as the AVI-1790-8 fuel-injected engine, larger fuel tanks, and a constant-pressure hydraulic system for the gun-control system, along with improvements to the suspension.

An improved version of the M48A2, the M48A2C, which can be identified externally by the omission of the track-tensioning idlers below the sprockets, saw service in Vietnam. The M48 variant most often associated with its service in Vietnam, however, is the M48A3.

With the production of the M60 Main Battle Tank in the late 1950s and its deployment in Europe, programs began to modernize huge fleet of M48 tanks. The 90mm gun was considered to be adequate for use in Vietnam where tank-to-tank combat was rare, and huge stockpiles of ammunition were on hand. Thus the decision was made to retain that weapon. Thus in 1967, conversion of M48A1s to the M48A3 began by installing the diesel powerpack of the M60 family along with other upgrades. The most noticeable external characteristic of the new variant is the tall vision ring below the commander's cupola. The M48A3 soon became the primary US tank in Vietnam.

M67A2

The M67 flamethrower tank, based on the M48A1, was procured by the US Marine Corps in the mid-1950s. As the M48A2 tank became available, an improved version of flamethrower tank was designed; thirty-five of the M67A1 were produced. With the advent of the M48A3, a flame tank based on that variant was introduced, the M67A2. Seventy-three M67A2 vehicles were produced.

The main armament for all variants was the M7A1-6 flamethrower, which consisted of the M7 fuel and pressure system and the M6 flame gun. The M6 flame gun on the M67 was installed in a housing visually similar to the standard 90mm gun. This was fitted with a fake bore evacuator and muzzle brake. The housing was shorter and slightly thicker in diameter than the actual 90mm gun. The pressurized fuel for the flamethrower was stored in tanks in the turret.

The first use of flame tanks in Vietnam was in August 1965 during Operation Starlite, and they were later used during Operation Dozer and the Battle of Hue.

GENERAL DATA

MODEL	M48A2C	M48A3	M67A1
WEIGHT^	105000	104000	104000
LENGTH*	342	342	342
WIDTH*	143	143	143
HEIGHT*	121.625	121.625	121.625
STD TRACK WIDTH	28	28	28
CREW	4	4	4
MAX SPEED	30 mph	30 mph	30 mph
FUEL CAPY	335 gallons	385 gallons	335 gallons
RANGE	160 miles	300 miles	160 miles
ELECTRICAL	24 negative	24 negative	24 negative
TRANSMISSION SPEEDS	2F 1R	2F 1R	2F 1R
TURNING RADIUS FEET	PIVOT	PIVOT	PIVOT
ARMAMENT MAIN SECONDARY FLEXIBLE	1x 90mm 1x .30 cal. 1x .50 cal.	1x 90mm 1x .30 cal. 1x .50 cal.	flamethrower 1x .30 cal. 1x .50 cal.

* Overall dimensions listed in inches. Measure with main gun facing forward, and anti-aircraft machine gun mounted.
^ Fighting weight.

ENGINE DATA

ENGINE MAKE/MODEL	Continental AVI-1790-8	Continental AVDSI-1790-2
NUMBER OF CYLINDERS	90 degree V-12	90 degree V-12
CUBIC INCH DISPLACEMENT	1791.75	1791.75
HORSEPOWER	825 @ 2800	750 @ 2400
TORQUE	1670 @ 2200	1710 @ 1800

The M48A2 was standardized in October of 1955, and began production two months later. This was an improved version of the M48 Patton that incorporated numerous improvements on the initial design. The raised rear deck was added to limit the tank's thermal signature, and the engine was the new fuel-injected gasoline AVI-1790-8. Other improvements included suspension revisions, increased fuel capacity, and a new hydraulic gun control system.

An improved version of the M48A2, the M48A2C, also saw combat in Vietnam, and is recognizable by the omission of the small track tensioning idler wheel below the drive sprocket behind the sixth road-wheel station. The bore evacuator of this M48A2C is marked with the nickname 'Wild One III', and the registration number 9B0311 is visible on the fender-mounted storage boxes. C-ration boxes are stored on the fenders and turret roof, and the foul weather cover is mounted on the gun mantlet. (*Chris Harlow*)

'Willie', an M48A2C of Troop A, 4th Battalion, 4th Cavalry, 1st Infantry Division, patrols a section of Highway 1 with an ACAV M113 APC late in August of 1968. The Xenon searchlight with its canvas cover is fitted above the main gun. The .50 cal. machine gun has been moved to a mount on the exterior of the cupola. This was a frequent modification in Vietnam that provided the commander better vision and field of fire while using the weapon. (*National Archives*)

A program to modernize the aging fleet of M48 tanks was developed with the introduction of the M60 MBT in the early 1960s. Conversions of M48A1 tanks began in 1963 and incorporated numerous upgrades, including the new AVDS-1790 diesel engine of the M60. The result of this program was the M48A3, recognizable by the air filter boxes on the rear fenders associated with the new engine. (*Patton Museum*)

The crew of 'Chaplain's Worry', an M48A3 registration number 9A8652, takes a break while on security duty on RT. 13 near Ben Cat, South Vietnam in May 1968. Spare track mounted to the turret sides serve a dual purpose, affording some degree of additional protection from RPGs and for repairs of mine damage. The lower suspension is covered in the common red dust of the region. The commander's machine gun has been relocated to the cupola roof. (*Office of History, US Army Corps of Engineers*)

Stationed on the perimeter of Fire Base Bastogne, an M48A3 crew awaits a convoy to escort into the base on 16 April 1968. The nickname 'Claustrophobia' is painted on the turret side in half red and white lettering, partially obscured by the machine gun ammunition boxes stowed on the turret grab-handles. The power connection for the searchlight is visible just above the name. The crew's personal items stored on the turret rear includes an orange and white civilian plastic ice chest. (*National Archives*)

An M48A3 with stacks of ration boxes, ammunition boxes, and track links added to the turret for extra protection sweeps a former Vietcong bunker complex. The tank is a part of 3rd Squadron, 11th Armored Cavalry Regiment operating north of Fire Base Bandit II in late November 1970. (*National Archives*)

An M48A3 equipped with the Earth Moving Blade M8 is nicknamed 'Charlie Brown,' with an image of the popular cartoon character on the turret side. The crew has paused on Route 79 near Ben Cat in June 1968. Spare road wheels and track are carried on the turret in readiness for ever-likely mine damage to a vehicle. The GI at the rear of the vehicle bears witness to the mine threat, his hand-held mine detector leaning against the tank. (*Office of History, US Army Corps of Engineers*)

Mine rollers were used on M48 tanks in Vietnam, the weight of the rollers exploding mines ahead of the vehicle. The mine roller on this M48A2 nicknamed 'Bandit' was made up from sheep's foot construction compactor rollers. Along with rollers, mine plows were also used, which dug below the mine and swept them to the side of the tank's path. (*Office of History, US Army Corps of Engineers*)

A variant of the M48A3 used in Vietnam by the Marine Corps was the M67A2 Flame Tank, which housed a flame projector disguised to look like the standard 90mm gun barrel. The flame gun had a range of elevation of +45 to -12 degrees, the depression being lower than the standard gun tank. A means of identifying an M67 is the flattened tops of the headlight guards that allowed clearance of the depressed gun. (*Patton Museum*)

Seventy-three M67A2s were produced, this vehicle belonging to the 1st Marine Division in Vietnam in 1968. The firing of both the flame projector and the coaxial 7.62mm machine gun were controlled by the gunner, who sighted through an XM30 periscopic sight, which provided a 48-degree field of vision and 1.5X magnification. (*Patton Museum*)

The M67A2 equipped with the M7A1-6 flame projector had a flame range of 280 yards (256 meters) operating at 300 psi with a 7/8-inch nozzle. Unlike the 90mm gun tank the M67A2 required no loader, giving the tank a crew of three. The loader's roof hatch was used to access the flamethrowers fuel tanks. Note the .30 cal. Browning MG mounted on the commander's cupola, and intercom speaker. (*Patton Museum*)

AVLB

While the concept of armored-vehicle-launched bridges (AVLB) dated back to the 1940s, it would be Vietnam before large-scale use of the equipment in combat situations by US troops began. AVLBs built on both the M48 and the later M60 chassis were used in Vietnam. Each AVLB carried a 63-foot aluminum folding bridge with a capacity of 63 tons.

For transport, the scissors bridge was folded, and rested on the bridge seat, above the rear of the engine deck of the tank chassis. At the front of the vehicle was a boom, outrigger and tongue, along with big hydraulic cylinders which deployed and withdrew the bridge. As the hydraulic cylinders extended the bridge, the boom and outrigger assemblies supported the rear of the bridge. Fixed-length cables in the scissors bridge acted to pull it open when it was being lowered into position. The bridge could be retrieved from either end. The bridge had a roadway width of 12½ feet. It took the two-man crew of the AVLB between 2 and 5 minutes to emplace the bridge, and about 10 minutes to retrieve it, with armor protection.

The M48 AVLB mounted a 63-foot assault bridge and deployment equipment upon the chassis of the M48A2 tank. Here seen as the vehicle begins deployment to place the bridge alongside a second span seen to the left of the photo. The bridge could be set in place in less than 10 minutes. (*Kevin Emdee collection*)

The M48 AVLB can be distinguished from the M60 variant by the track tensioning roller wheel between the final road wheel and the drive sprocket, and a lack of air cleaner boxes on the fenders. The rear bracing for the weight of the bridge unit is mounted at the rear of the tank above the engine deck. (*Kevin Emdee collection*)

The same vehicle is seen as it proceeds with emplacement of the assault bridge. The two-section scissor-bridge weighed in excess of 14 tons and was operated hydraulically from within the protection of the tank chassis' armor . Once deployed the chassis could quickly detach from the bridge, allowing other vehicles to cross. The bridge could be recovered from either end of the span. (*Kevin Emdee collection*)

Here the same bridging unit is seen on the chassis of the M60 tank. Designated as M60 AVLB, these units also saw service in Vietnam. The same engine was used as that of the M48A3, simplifying supply chain issues. The bridge unit was constructed of aluminum for weight savings and was capable of supporting 60-ton vehicles, ample for the M48 tanks used in the Vietnam War. (*Chris Harlow*)

The scissor-bridge is extended forward of this M60 AVLB (US Army Number 9B8138) at a base in Vietnam. The mechanism of the launcher assembly can be seen with its two massive hydraulic cylinders and base plate or outrigger that steadies the unit as it is deployed or recovered. The bridge has perhaps been deployed here for practice or to reduce the load on the vehicle's suspension. (*Chris Harlow*)

The M60 AVLBs were a great asset to units in South Vietnam, due to the terrain and the amount of rainfall. Here a road is cleared of vehicles to move the bridging equipment forward to span some obstacle. The driver's position was moved to the turret ring area of the chassis, and the former position was used for the hydraulic equipment. (*William Powis*)

A similar scene, as ACAV M113s exit the road to move the M60 AVLB forward to get the unit moving again. In the original print a depression is evident forward of the line of vehicles to the left of the muddy road. (*William Powis*)

An ironic situation, an M60 AVLB sits mired in water and mud up to the upper run of tracks, a state the vehicle was designed to help other vehicles avoid. The M60 AVLB has had a long service life with US forces, with a number of M60A2 chassis converted through the late 1990s, some fitted with a heavier bridge capable of supporting 70 tons. (*William Powis*)

M728 Combat Engineer Vehicle

Based on the M60A1 medium tank chassis, the M728 Combat Engineer Vehicle was a workhorse CEV equipped with an A-frame boom and winch attached to the turret and a bulldozer blade mounted on the front of the hull.

The M728 was armed with a short-barreled 165mm M135 gun which was used for demolition purposes. Stowed aboard were thirty rounds of high-explosive, plastic (HEP) ammunition. Typical uses of the vehicle were blasting or bulldozing obstacles, recovering other vehicles, and general hoisting/lifting operations.

The A-frame boom was mounted on, and pivoted on, tubular supports that jutted from both sides of the turret. The A-frame boom could hoist 17,500 pounds with a single line. The winch was mounted on the center rear of the turret. It had a pulling capacity of 25,000 pounds in a straight pull.

Production of the M728 Combat Engineer Vehicle began in 1966, 243 being manufactured through 1972. Its turret mounted boom had a lifting capacity of 17,500 pounds, was hydraulically operated with 360 degree traverse and a two speed hydraulic winch. The short barreled 165mm M135 gun was used for demolition purposes, and the 146" wide bulldozer blade was used for clearing obstacles. (*TACOM LCMC History Office*)

An M728 of the 26th Engineer Battalion passes through Landing Zone Fat Boy in South Vietnam on 7 November 1968. The M728 was based on the M60A1 gun tank with its A-frame boom pivoted on tubular supports that protrude from both sides of the turret. The position of the headlights and guards are raised to allow clearance over the dozer blade in the raised traveling position. (*National Archives*)

The powerpack (engine/transmission assembly) is being removed from an M728 by a maintenance crew using an M543 5-ton wrecker. The turret is traversed 90 degrees to clear access to the engine deck. Although the M728 was based on the M60 chassis, the powerpack was common with the M48A3. (*Chris Harlow*)

M578 recovery vehicle G-309

Developed by FMC as an air-transportable heavy lifting crane for barrel replacements of self-propelled guns of the M107/M110 family, the M578 served more as a wrecker and a general recovery vehicle. The new recovery vehicle cab on a modified M107/110 SPG chassis was originally known as the T120. The T120 developed into the T120E1 and finally the M578 Light Armored Full Tracked Recovery Vehicle and was primarily built by Bowen-McLaughlin-York.

The M578 hull is essentially the same as the chassis used for the M107/110 Self-Propelled Gun with the engine mounted to the right and the driver on the left, separated by a insulated metal firewall. Powering the generator and the hydraulic pumps when the main engine is shut off is an auxiliary drive directly behind the power plant. The winches, boom, cab, and rear spade are powered by hydraulic pumps.

During recovery operations the crew controlled the winches and boom from inside the turret cab. The M578 was equipped with two hydraulically powered winches, a 30,000lb boom winch and a 60,000lb drag winch. The boom winch was a two-speed unit fitted with 5/8-inch cable and an internal automatic brake allowing the load to remain suspended while the engine was off. The boom elevation cylinders penetrate the front turret wall and attached to the boom just forward of the cab.

Behind the crane operator's seat was a full height tool locker for recovery gear and tools, accessible from outside the crane cab. The hull and turret cab of the M578 were constructed of welded steel armor plate, providing protection from small arms fire and shell splinters. The armor could not withstand a hit from any modern tank or artillery. An M2 .50 cal. Browning machine gun was mounted on a pintle on the cab roof near the cupola.

The Detroit Diesel GMC 8V71T turbo-supercharged eight-cylinder, V-type 2 cycle diesel, driving through an Allison model XTG-411-2A Crossdrive transmission, made up the powerpack of the M578.

GENERAL DATA

MODEL	M578
WEIGHT	54000
LENGTH*	250.25
WIDTH*	124
HEIGHT*	130.5
MAX SPEED	37 mph
FUEL CAPY	320 gallons
RANGE	450 miles
ELECTRICAL	24 negative

* Overall dimensions listed in inches. Measure with main gun facing forward, and anti-aircraft machine gun mounted.

ENGINE DATA

ENGINE MAKE/MODEL*	GM 8V71T
NUMBER OF CYLINDERS	V-8
HORSEPOWER	345 @ 2300 rpm

The M578 Armored Recovery Vehicle was based on the hull and suspension of the M107/M110 self-propelled howitzer. The cab that housed the boom and winches rotated like a turret and reversed from this view for travel. The spade seen lowered here braced the vehicle for heavy pulls, the winch that routed through the boom having a 30,000 pound pull capacity; the second winch had a 60,000-pound capacity. (*US Army photo*)

Members of the 140th Maintenance Battalion use the boom of their M578 to assist in changing the 175mm gun tube of an M107 self-propelled howitzer. The howitzer is attached to Battery A, 7th Battalion, 8Th Artillery, II Field Force operating near Bien Hoa South Vietnam on 24 November 1969. (*US Army photo*)

The same vehicles are seen from the previous photo, as their work continues. The second boom of the 5-ton wrecker is used to balance the gun tube as the chassis of the M107 is pulled forward, freeing the tube. The roof of the cab of the M578 ARV is equipped with an ACAV-style shield for its M2 .50 cal. machine gun that is missing from the pintle mount. (*US Army photo*)

M88 G-298

The M88 was developed to support the M48 family of vehicles. This vehicle combined the power plant of the M51, suspension components of the M48, and an all-new hull and recovery system. The vehicle was developed by Bowen-McLaughlin-York Inc., of York, Pennsylvania, and they were awarded a contract to produce 1,075 units in 1959. The original M88 was gasoline powered and was deployed during the Vietnam War.

During the 1970s, the Army began developing an all-diesel vehicle fleet. Thus the M88 retrievers received new diesel powerplants. At the time of the conversion a diesel-powered Auxiliary Power Unit (APU) was installed. The new diesel-powered retriever is recognizable by the APU's grille just behind the right-side door of the retriever, and was classified as the M88A1.

Two hydraulically powered winches – one to operate the hoist, and a massive 90,000-lbs capacity main recovery winch – occupy the lower portion of the cast-armor hull. The main recovery winch is mounted near the front of the vehicle. Its drum contains 200 feet of 1.25-inch diameter cable. A hydraulically operated A-frame boom is used with the hoisting winch and is equipped with 400 feet of 5/8-inch wire rope. With the front ground spade lowered the winch has a 50,000-lbs. capacity. Mounted near the center of the vehicle, beneath the floor plates is the hoist winch. The vehicles were fitted with various equipment include a hydraulically driven, heavy-duty impact wrench, a hydraulically operated refueling pump, and the bow-mounted blade. The blade was to be used to stabilize the vehicle during heavy lifts, and as a ground anchor during heavy winching operations. It could also be used for light earthwork in conjunction with recovery operations. It was specifically not for use in heavy earth moving such as preparing defensive positions, although photographs exist of the vehicles being used in this manner.

GENERAL DATA

MODEL	M88
WEIGHT^	112000
LENGTH*	325.5
WIDTH*	135
HEIGHT*	115
MAX SPEED	30 mph
FUEL CAPY	445 gallons
RANGE	222 miles
ELECTRICAL	24 negative
TURNING RADIUS FEET	PIVOT

* Overall dimensions listed in inches.

^ Fighting weight.

ENGINE DATA

ENGINE MAKE/MODEL	Continental AVSI-1790-6
NUMBER OF CYLINDERS	90 degree V-12
CUBIC INCH DISPLACEMENT	1790
HORSEPOWER	1020 @ 2800
TORQUE	1900 @ 2200
GOVERNED SPEED (rpm)	2800

The M88 Armored Recovery Vehicle went into production in 1961 and is based on the chassis of the M48 tank. Its winch is capable of a single line 70-ton recovery, or up to a 140-ton recovery using 140-ton pulley and a double line. The vehicle is equipped with a boom that can accomplish a 35-ton lift. As of this printing a variant, the M88A2, is still in service with the US army. (*TACOM LCMC History Office*)

The M88's blade was not designed for bulldozing, and such use as this could severely damage the vehicle. This M88 is digging an emplacement for Troop B, 3rd Battalion, 4th Cavalry northwest of Saigon during January of 1967. The improvised gun shield on the roof is marked with the nickname 'Big Boss Man', and appears to be painted a darker color than the rest of the vehicle. (*National Archives*)

Members of Troop A, 1st Squadron, 10th Cavalry train personnel of 3rd ARVN Cavalry on the use of the M88 on 27 October 1970. The boom is being used to pull the engine and radiator assembly from an ACAV M113. The bow of the M88 is littered with chains, and spare track and return rollers are carried on the hull side. (*National Archives*)

An M88 crew prepares to recover an M48A3 (not visible) of Company M, 3rd Squadron, 11th Armored Cavalry Regiment, from a stream bed in late November 1970 near Fire Support Base Bandit II. The vehicle carries a spare road wheel, track return roller and drive sprocket, which would often be damaged by mines on the vehicle or on M48 tanks they serviced. (*National Archives*)

A mine-damaged M48A3 is loaded onto a M15A2 semi-trailer coupled to a 10-ton dual winch truck-tractor, lifted by the booms of two M88 armored recovery vehicles. This is part of a retrograde action during the draw down of US troops in Vietnam at Da Nang on 8 November 1971. (*National Archives*)

M51 G-274

The development of the T43/M103 family of 120mm gun-armed heavy tanks, fielded in the 1950s, required comparably large and powerful recovery vehicles. This requirement resulted in the M51. Although the service life of the tanks quickly ended with the Army, they remained in service with the Marines. The Marine Corps did not deploy the M103 to Vietnam, but as their primary tank recovery vehicle, the M51 did see service during the war.

Produced by Chrysler at the Detroit Tank Arsenal, a pilot model of the vehicle, designated T51, began testing at Aberdeen Proving Ground in April 1953. The vehicle proved largely satisfactory during trials, and series production soon began. The most visible differences between the two test examples and production vehicles was the deletion of rear outriggers which were replaced by a blade, similar to the one on the front of the vehicle. These blades were used to stabilize the vehicle during recovery and lifting operations. The vehicles were equipped with a hydraulically driven 45-ton capacity recovery winch as well as a five-ton capacity auxiliary winch.

Chrysler built 187 of the vehicles in 1954–1955, which were standardized as the M51. Both the Army and Marines initially used the M51, but the Marines continued using the vehicle long after the Army had switched to the M88. Unlike the M103 heavy tank, the M51 never received a Diesel conversion.

GENERAL DATA

MODEL	M51
WEIGHT^	120000
LENGTH*	399
WIDTH*	143
HEIGHT*	129
MAX SPEED	30 mph
FUEL CAPY	400 gallons
RANGE	200 miles
ELECTRICAL	24 negative
TORQMATIC TRANSMISSION SPEEDS	3
TURNING RADIUS FEET	PIVOT

* Overall dimensions listed in inches.

^ Fighting weight.

ENGINE DATA

ENGINE MAKE/MODEL	Continental AVSI-1790-6
NUMBER OF CYLINDERS	90 degree V-12
CUBIC INCH DISPLACEMENT	1790
HORSEPOWER	1020 @ 2800
TORQUE	1900 @ 2200
GOVERNED SPEED (rpm)	2800

The Recovery Vehicle, Heavy, M51 was based on the chassis of the M103 Heavy Tank, and at over 30 feet long and 60 tons was the heaviest and largest vehicle fielded in Vietnam by US forces. The vehicles were deployed for tank recovery by the USMC. It was equipped with spades at the front and rear to assist in recovery operations. (*TACOM LCMC History Office*)

An M51 has its crane boom raised and traversed to the left side. The spades on the front and rear were operated by cables from an auxiliary winch mounted within the cab. This massive vehicle's tracks were T107 type with rubber blocks that were 28 inches wide to provide adequate flotation. (*Patton Museum*)

Repairs are made to the left final drive of an M51 at the USMC base at Dong Ha, South Vietnam in 1968. The drive sprocket is laying on the ground between the retriever and the wrecker. A heavy-duty tow bar is stowed on the left rear fender. Note the crane hooks of both the vehicles are painted yellow and black for caution, and the overall color of the vehicles is darker than Olive Drab. (*National Archives*)

An M51 uses its heavy duty tow bar, missing from its mounts on the right-rear fender, to push an M48 forward on a tank transporter at the 1st Force Service Regiment base, Da Nang, in December 1967. The boom of the crane is in the extended position on the vehicle. (*National Archives*)

The heavy rains of South Vietnam often made the use of tracked vehicles precarious. Here an M51 armored recovery vehicle churns through the soupy mud at a USMC base at Con Thien, Republic of Vietnam, during December of 1967. Its aim is to extract the M50 Ontos visible ahead and to the right of the M51 (*National Archives*)

Self-propelled Weapons

M53 155mm Self-propelled Gun SNL G-259

The M53 155mm self-propelled gun was one of the largest vehicles fielded by the US military in Vietnam. First used by US troops during the 1950s, the M53, and its sister vehicle, the M55 8-inch self-propelled howitzer, were developed by Pacific Car and Foundry, utilizing the automotive components of the Patton tank. The M53 was powered by the AV-1790-7B engine and CD-850-4B transmission

At the rear of the chassis, a large limited-traverse turret provided the mounting for the M46 155mm cannon, while on the M55 the turret housed an 8-inch howitzer. A crew of six men operated the vehicle, all in the turret. These included the driver at turret front-left, section chief, gunner and the three cannoneers. Provisions were made for stowage of twenty main gun rounds.

While the Army converted its M53s to M55s during the 1950s, the Marines continued to use the M53, including service in the early days of the Corps operations in Vietnam. In 1969 the Marines phased out the M53 in favor of the M107.

GENERAL DATA

MODEL	**M53**
WEIGHT^	96000
MAX TOWED LOAD	5000
LENGTH*	402
WIDTH*	133
HEIGHT*	137
STD TRACK WIDTH	23 inches
MAX SPEED	30 mph
FUEL CAPY	380 gallons
RANGE	160 miles
ELECTRICAL	24 negative
TRANSMISSION SPEEDS	2
TURNING RADIUS FEET	PIVOT

* Overall dimensions listed in inches. Measure with main gun facing forward, and anti-aircraft machine gun mounted.

^ Fighting weight.

ENGINE DATA

ENGINE MAKE/MODEL*	Continental AV-1790-5B,5C,5D
NUMBER OF CYLINDERS	90 Degree V
CUBIC INCH DISPLACEMENT	1791.75
HORSEPOWER	704 @ 2800
TORQUE	1440 @ 2000
GOVERNED SPEED	2800

G-295 M107 175mm self propelled gun and M110 8-inch self-propelled howitzer

Both the M107 and M110 shared the same chassis; the difference between models was strictly in armament. The vehicles were equipped with torsion bar suspension with five dual rubber-tired roadwheels on each side. The drive sprockets were at the front, and the last road wheel acted as the idler. There were no track return rollers. A Detroit Diesel Model 8V-71T diesel engine driving through an Allison Transmission XTG-411-2A cross-drive transmission at the front of the hull made up the vehicle's powerpack.

Pacific Car and Foundry began deliveries of the M107 175mm self-propelled gun in 1962. The weapon was mounted on a large rotating platform at the rear of the open vehicle. The mount could traverse 30 degrees either side of center, and the gun elevated to 65 degrees. The weapon was served by a crew of thirteen, five of which rode on the M107, the remainder in an accompanying M548 ammo carrier. The vehicle was anchored during firing by a spade at the rear of the hull. FMC and Bowen-McLaughlin-York produced the M107 in later years. The M107 was used extensively in Vietnam for long-range bombardment, having a maximum firing range of roughly 20 miles, and a projectile weighing about 175 pounds.

The M110, the 8-inch-howitzer armed version, was also produced by Pacific Car and Foundry concurrently with the M107. Later production, like the M107, was also by FMC and BMY. Also used extensively in Vietnam, its range was only about half that of the M107. With a 200-pound round, its reputation was for greater accuracy and ease of use than the 175mm round.

The M110 was replaced in 1976 by the M110A1, its much longer barrel giving it increased range. Later, with the addition of a muzzle brake allowing an increase of powder charge, the range was further increased. The self-propelled howitzers with the new muzzle brake were known as M110A2, and all the US Army and Marine Corps M107s were rearmed with the weapon.

Tipping the scales at over 90,000-pounds, the M53 155mm self-propelled gun and the M55 8-inch self-propelled howitzer were among the largest vehicles fielded by the US military during the Cold War and Vietnam War era. The M53, shown here, can be distinguished from the M55 most readily by looking at the length of the gun tube. The M53's 155mm barrel extends beyond the end of the hull as seen here, whereas the 8-inch armed M55 does not. (*Patton Museum*)

Marines of the 3rd Marine Division dispatch a 155mm round on an enemy position at Phu Bai on 7 February 1967. (*USMC via Steve Zaloga*)

GENERAL DATA

MODEL	M107	M110
WEIGHT^	62100	58500
LENGTH*	444.8	294.4
WIDTH*	124	124
HEIGHT*	136.8	115.6
CREW	5	5
MAX SPEED	34 mph	34 mph
FUEL CAPY	300 gallons	300 gallons
RANGE	450 miles	450 miles
ELECTRICAL	24V negative	24V negative
TRANSMISSION SPEEDS	4F 2R	4F 2R
TURNING RADIUS FEET	PIVOT	PIVOT
ARMAMENT MAIN	175mm	8 inch

* Overall dimensions listed in inches. Measured with main gun facing forward, and anti-aircraft machine gun mounted.
^ Fighting weight.

ENGINE DATA

ENGINE MAKE/MODEL*	GM 8V71T
NUMBER OF CYLINDERS	8
CUBIC INCH DISPLACEMENT	567.4
HORSEPOWER	345 @ 2300
TORQUE	980 @ 1700

The M107 175mm self-propelled gun was developed in the 1950s to replace the M55 8-inch self-propelled howitzer. The M55 weighed in at 44 tons and was not air-transportable. The M107 production models weighed 28.3 tons, and with its 405 horsepower turbocharged diesel engine was capable of a top speed of 30 mph on roads. The vehicle incorporated innovations in suspension and gun laying systems that improved accuracy compared to previous weapons. (*US Army*)

An M107 175mm self-propelled gun fires a shell during Operation San Angelo on 27 January 1968. The gun was capable of firing a shell out to a maximum range of 22 miles with a blast circumference of up to 250 yards. The length of the barrel was approx. 34½ ft. (*National Archives*)

'Proud American' an M107 of 2nd Battery, 32nd Artillery, II Field Force has its barrel changed by members of the 94th Maintenance Company in Doc Lap, Republic of Vietnam, on 23 November 1969. The two 5-ton wreckers balance the gun barrel while the chassis of the vehicle is driven away. Early barrels were limited to approx. 300 rounds before needing to be re-tubed. (*National Archives*)

The M110 self-propelled 8-inch howitzer was developed in conjunction with the M107 and began production in the late 1950s. The 8-inch howitzer had a significantly shorter range than the 175mm gun, but a higher rate of fire could be sustained when using the manual hand-held rammer. The M110 and M107 shared all suspension and automotive components. (*TACOM LCMC History Office*)

A gunner of Battery C, 7th Battalion, 8th Artillery, with his hands on the lanyard fires an 8-inch round from an M110 in Vietnam on 8 August 1969. American artillery units were very formidable forces during the Vietnam War. (*National Archives*)

A member of 548 Light Maintenance Company, 277th Supply and Service Battalion, 29th General Support Group, stands in the empty engine bay of an M110 in South Vietnam on 19 April 1970. The M110 was powered by the Detroit Diesel 8V71T, turbocharged 8 cylinder Diesel engine producing 405 horsepower. (*National Archives*)

M108 and M109

In 1953 the Army began developing a new generation of self-propelled howitzer which would be a purpose-built vehicle, rather than the adapted tank chassis used on previous such vehicles. Initial efforts with this new generation of vehicle were the T195 armed with a 110mm weapon, and the T196 with a 156mm; by 1956, however, the conventional bores of 105mm and 155mm were approved. The pilot model of the T195 had been finished in the fall of 1958, the T196 pilot following in March 1959. Two of the four pilot models were repowered with diesel engines in 1960 and were designated as T195E1 and T196E1. Due to serious shortcomings in suspension and power train, two all-new pilots were tested in 1961, with the results being favorable.

Production began in 1962, and in July 1963 the vehicles were classified as standard. The 105mm-armed version was designated M108, and the 155mm-armed version as the M109.

M108 production totaled just over 350 units and ended in 1963. The Army favored the more powerfully armed M109 and its production continued until 1969. Depending upon the contract and year of manufacture, the builders were Cadillac Motor Car division of General Motors, Chrysler Corporation, and Allison Division of General Motors, but all the M109s were built in the Cleveland tank plant.

A total of 1,961 M109s were purchased by the US Army, with 150 more bought by the Marine Corps. The vehicles proved themselves well with both branches in Vietnam. It was shown that the M109, armed with the T255E4 155mm weapon, when firing the XM1119 propellant charge for maximum range caused damage to both the vehicle and crew. A longer barreled XM185 weapon was tested in 1969. The results proved satisfactory, and very little modification to the vehicle was necessary to install this new weapon, with the resultant vehicle being designated M109A1.

GENERAL DATA

MODEL	M108	M109
WEIGHT^	46221	52461
LENGTH*	240.7	260.4
WIDTH*	124	124
HEIGHT*	129.1	129.1
CREW	5	6
MAX SPEED	35 mph	35 mph
FUEL CAPY	135 gallons	135 gallons
RANGE	220 miles	220 miles
ELECTRICAL	24V negative	24V negative
TRANSMISSION SPEEDS	4F 2R	4F 2R
TURNING RADIUS FEET	PIVOT	PIVOT
ARMAMENT MAIN FLEXIBLE	105mm 1x .50	155mm 1x .50

* Overall dimensions listed in inches. Measured with main gun facing forward, and anti-aircraft machine gun mounted.
^ Fighting weight.

ENGINE DATA

ENGINE MAKE/MODEL*	GM 8V71T
NUMBER OF CYLINDERS	8
CUBIC INCH DISPLACEMENT	567.4
HORSEPOWER	345 @ 2300
TORQUE	980 @ 1700

The M109 self-propelled 155mm howitzer was put into production in 1963 with the weapon housed in a lightly armored turret at the rear of the chassis. The vehicle shared the Detroit Diesel 8V71T engine with the M107 and M110. The M109 is easily recognized by its short barrel with large double baffle muzzle brake and large fume extractor. The M109 had a maximum range of approximately 9 miles. (*National Archives*)

Members of Battalion Maintenance prepare to disconnect the powerpack on an M109 155mm self-propelled howitzer of Battery B, 13th Artillery in Vietnam on 30 September 1969. Tremendous assets were committed to the Army and Marine Corps to keep vehicles and equipment repaired and maintained in the combat zones during the Vietnam war. (*National Archives*)

Soldiers perform engine maintenance on an M109 of Battery A, 2nd battalion, 35th Artillery on 2 September 1970. Battery A had been detached to provide fire support for an Australian Task Force operating in the area. (*National Archives*)

An M109's (US Army number 12A45865) gun is at full elevation in a prepared emplacement in overlooking a valley in South Vietnam. The nickname 'Cong Coffee' is painted on the upper edge of the turret front, referring to unique Vietnamese style coffee. The gun position is ringed with dugouts and huts with their roofs protected from air-burst artillery by sandbags. (*Patton Museum*)

Towed Weapons

The M55 Quad mount

Developed during World War II, the M55 Multiple Caliber .50 Machine Gun Mount was itself an outgrowth of the M33 twin .50 caliber mount designed by the W.L. Maxson Company. The M33 had been created in response to the US Army's desire for a multiple machine gun air defense system.

The turret of the M55 was operated electrically; the power was supplied by batteries, which in turn were charged by a 300-watt generator, itself driven by a Briggs and Stratton gasoline engine.

These weapons were again used in World War II as well as in Korea, and continued to be issued for many years thereafter. Through time, however, the mounts, modified well beyond their serviceable age with the original Briggs and Stratton engines, were replaced with new 'Military Standard' engines. Also eschewed were the tombstone-shaped ammo boxes common during World War II with standard rectangular ammunition boxes being used instead.

Each of the Air Defense Artillery Battalions that were deployed to Vietnam included in their Table of Organization and Equipment a battery of M55 quad mounts. In accordance with the TOE, these mounts were initially installed in a 2½-ton truck using a Loading Aid Kit 7069664.

Battery G, 65th Artillery and Battery D, 71st Artillery, were the first of the type to deploy to Vietnam, arriving in November 1966. They were joined by Battery E, 41st Artillery, arriving in 11 March 1967, and Battery G, 55th Artillery, which was deployed 26 February 1968.

Although the Quad mounts were of little use against jet aircraft, they proved formidable weapons against ground targets, both in perimeter defense as well as convoy protection. Charles E. Kirkpatrick reported in the spring 1989 issue of *Vietnam* magazine that these units fired 10 million rounds of .50-caliber machine gun ammunition while in Vietnam.

The .50-caliber multiple gun carriages M55 was a powered, quadruple .50-caliber machine gun mount developed and put into service during World War II. Seen here is an example of a prototype version of that gun mount, designated the Multiple Caliber .50 Machine Gun Trailer Mount T81E1, comprising a Multiple Caliber .50 Machine Gun Mount M45E1 installed on a Mount Trailer T45E1. (*Rock Island Arsenal Museum*)

The .50-caliber multiple gun carriage M55 also went under such designations as the Quad .50-caliber Machine Gun M55 Mount, Trailer. This example, comprising an M45 mount on an M20 trailer, was photographed at the Rock Island Arsenal in Illinois in July 1967. (*Rock Island Arsenal Museum*)

A shield formed of thin armor provided some protection for the gunner. Attached to the trunnions above the upper machine guns are brackets holding a lateral rod to which the gun sight was attached. Various types of sights were available for use on this mount. (*Rock Island Arsenal Museum*)

The four Browning M2 HB .50-caliber machine guns of the M55 multiple gun carriage are at full elevation of 90 degrees. By the time of the Vietnam War, the US Army had re-placed the original 200-round, 89-pound, tombstone-shaped M2 ammunition chests with plain ammo boxes, as seen here. (*Rock Island Arsenal Museum*)

107mm M98 Howtar

Artillery support for troops operating in mountainous regions has been a problem since the advent of artillery. The US Army, among others, addressed this issue by having animals carry the artillery, rather than towing it. Development of the 75mm Pack Howitzer M1 began in 1920, and it was classified as Standard in 1927. The term 'pack' howitzer indicates that the weapon could be broken down to be transported in sections, often by mules during World War II. The M1A1, which had an improved breech, superseded it. Later versions used the M8 carriage with pneumatic wheels. During World War II, the Ordnance Department provided separate designations for guns and carriages. In 1962 the M1A1 howitzer on M8 carriage was re-designated the M116.

The US military considered the Pack Howitzer obsolete as a combat weapon by the time US involvement in Vietnam was peaking. However, a derivative, the M98 Howtar, was used in Vietnam by the Marines.

The M98 consisted of a 107mm M30 mortar tube installed in place of the howitzer tube of the M116. The 2nd Battalion, 13th Marines also used 107mm 'howtars,' which were a 4.2-inch mortar tube mounted on the carriage of the pack howitzer. Rock Island Arsenal carried out much of this conversion work.

GENERAL DATA

MODEL	M98
CALIBER	106MM/4.2 INCHES
RANGE	4,500 m max/515 m minimum
FIRING RATE	5 rpm for 20 minutes; 1 rpm indefinitely
ACTION	RECOIL
LENGTH	12 FT 3 INCHES
WEIGHT, TOWED	1,289 LBS

Designated the M98 Howtar, this weapon combined the potent but very heavy M30 107mm mortar tube with the proven carriage of the obsolete M1A1 Pack Howitzer. This example was photographed at Rock Island Arsenal, where it was developed. (*Rock Island Arsenal Museum*)

The M98 Howtar is most readily distinguished from the M1A1/M116 Pack Howitzer by the lack of a conventional breech. Here several of the weapons are displayed at Rock Island, illustrating the elevation range. (*Rock Island Arsenal Museum*)

A few of the M98s saw service in the early stages of the Vietnam fighting, and were capable of hurling a 9-pound projectile to a distance of over 2½ miles. (*National Archives*)

Throughout the twentieth century the Marine Corps often used equipment long considered obsolete by the US Army, as was the case with the M98. Here a Marine gunner of the 3rd Division takes coordinates for an indirect fire mission in South Vietnam in 1965. (*National Archives*)

M101A1 105mm Howitzer

The 105mm howitzer formed the backbone of US field artillery units during World War II. The definitive American 105 was the M2A1, which entered production in April 1941. In November 1942 the War Department policy changed such that towed-loads of fewer than 5,000 pounds were no longer required to have service brakes. A new carriage, the M2A1, was developed in response. The Carriage M2A2 featured an improved screw traverse mechanism, and more noticeably, a two-section gun shield. The M2A2 carriage is readily distinguished from the M2A1 by the addition of the auxiliary gun shield mounted in front of the primary shield. This carriage was introduced in August 1943. After World War II, the Howitzer 105mm M2A1 on Carriage M2A2 was re-designated the Howitzer 105mm M101A1, while the Howitzer 105mm M2A1 on Carriage M2 or M2A1 became known as the Howitzer 105mm M101. The howitzer has a maximum elevation of 1,180 mils (about 66 degrees) and a maximum range of 12,205 yards, which can be reached at an elevation of 778.6 mils with a maximum zone charge. Production of these weapons continued until 1953, and they saw widespread use in Vietnam.

GENERAL DATA

MODEL	M101A1
CALIBER	105mm
RANGE	7 miles
FIRING RATE	10 rpm max; 3 rpm sustained
MUZZLE VELOCITY	1,550 ft/s
LENGTH	19 FT 6 INCHES
WEIGHT, TOWED	4,980 lbs

A WWII veteran called upon for service in the Vietnam fighting is the M2A1 105mm Howitzer, re-designated M101A1 in 1962. Here a howitzer of H Company, 3rd 8-Inch Howitzer Battery, 1st Marine Division is set in place on a Fire Base during 1967. The M101A1 was still a formidable weapon at this time, with a high explosive projectile of over 30 lbs. and capable of a range of up to 7 miles. (*National Archives*)

An M101A1 howitzer of 'C' Battery, First Battalion, Eleventh Marines fires at enemy positions in South Vietnam in 1968. By this time the greatest attribute of the 105 howitzer was availability, with over 10,000 units having been produced when production ended at Rock Island Arsenal in 1953. (*National Archives*)

A Marine of Fire Support Base 'Alpine' puts finishing touches on a 105mm howitzer emplacement on 24 October 1968. The USMC marking on the recuperator assembly is stenciled in yellow. (*National Archives*)

Marines fire an M101A1 Howitzer from behind a sandbag emplacement in Vietnam in 1969. The guns were known for excellent accuracy and the rounds were powerful. The rounds could be handled by a single loader, and a well trained gun crew could have bursts of fire of up to ten rounds per minute, and sustained fire of three rounds per minute. (*National Archives*)

A gun crew of the 3rd Marine Division manually repositions an M101A1 105mm Howitzer at a Fire Support Base in Vietnam during 1968. A red and white striped aiming-stake is visible in the background, used by crews to ascertain the gun's position after firing to accurately aim indirect fire. (*National Archives*)

M114 155mm Howitzer

Developed during World War II under the designation 155mm Howitzer M1, this towed artillery piece entered production in October 1942. Its intended use was as a divisional artillery weapon. During World War II the howitzer was used by both the Army and the Marine Corps. It was re-designated the M114A1 in 1962.

GENERAL DATA

MODEL	M114
CALIBER	155mm
RANGE	16,000 yards
FIRING RATE	4 rpm max; 40 rph sustained
MUZZLE VELOCITY	1,847 ft/s
LENGTH	20 FT
WEIGHT, TOWED	12,800 lbs

The M114A1 155mm Howitzer, formerly known as M1A1 prior to 1962, was another piece of WWII equipment which saw extensive service in Vietnam. A gun crew of 3rd Battalion, 11th Regiment, 1st Marine Division prepares a howitzer for a fire mission in 1968. The two men at the rear between the split trails have just swabbed the bore with a cleaning sponge. (*National Archives*)

A view of 'Whiskey' Battery, 3rd Battalion, 11th Marine Regiment gives details of the construction and layout of the firing emplacement. It is ringed with a wall built from crates filled with earth, topped with sandbags. This protects both the crew and a ring of propellant charges for the rounds, seen forward and to the left of the gun. Each member of the crew wears the ubiquitous flak vest. (*National Archives*)